IMAGES
*of America*

# PARSONS

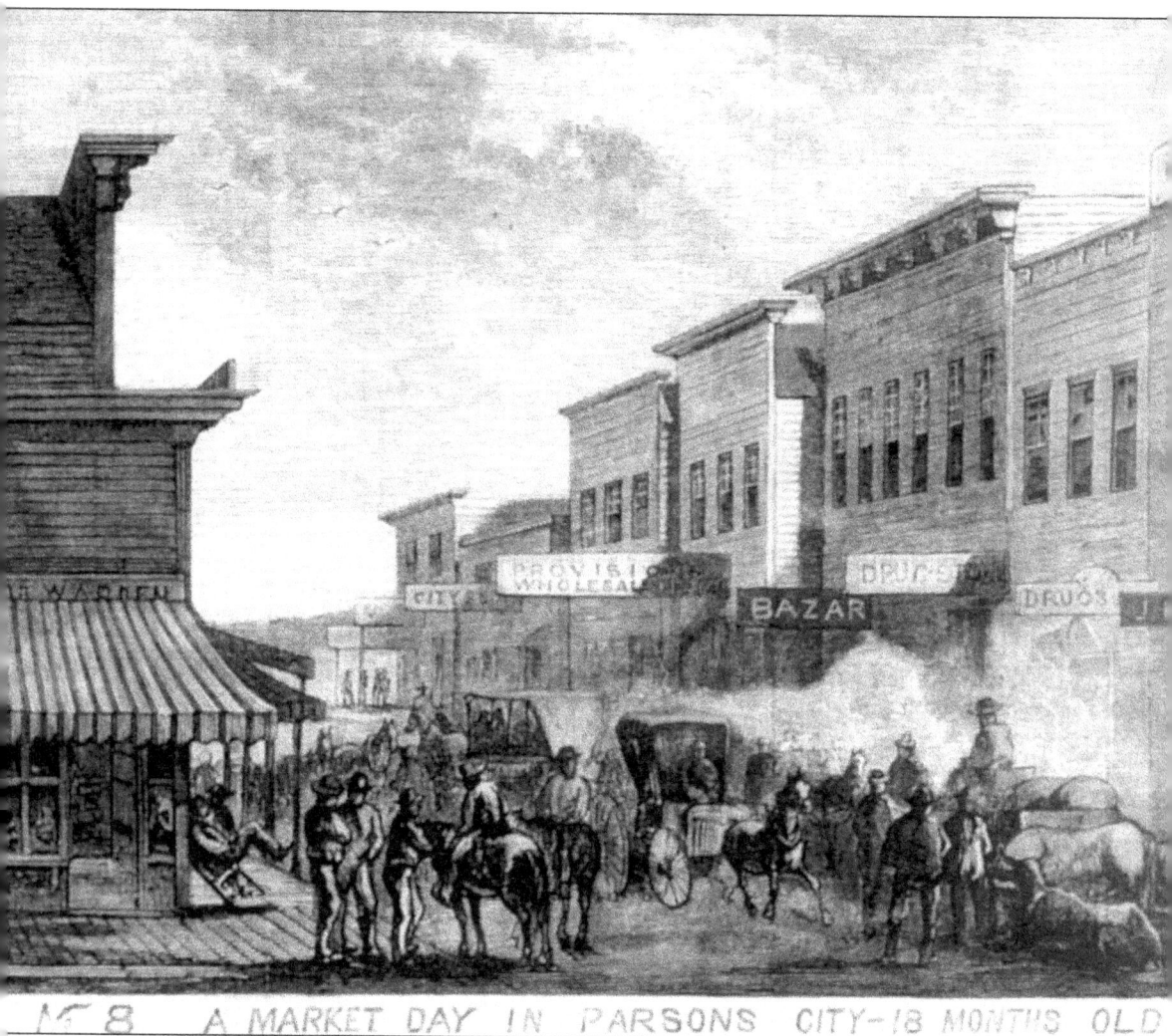

A MARKET DAY IN PARSONS CITY—18 MONTHS OLD

A picture of Parsons City appeared in the November 8, 1873, edition of *Harper's Weekly*. It was one of the first commercially produced images of the city. Based on drawings by artists who were sent to document "life out West," the market day engraving was one of several featured. Other images included "A Smoking City, Pittsburg," "Taking Water in the Prairie," and "Prairie Chickens for Sale."

*On the cover*: In 1911, members of the community enthusiastically greeted the circus that came to town. While many buildings in the business district have changed over the years, the ones on the south side of the 1700 block of Main Street remain much as they were almost 100 years ago. (Courtesy of the Iron Horse Historical Museum.)

IMAGES
*of America*

# PARSONS

David Mattox and Mike Brotherton

ARCADIA
PUBLISHING

Published by Arcadia Publishing
Charleston SC, Chicago IL, Portsmouth NH, San Francisco CA

Library of Congress Catalog Card Number: 2008926405

For all general information contact Arcadia Publishing at:
Telephone 843-853-2070
Fax 843-853-0044
E-mail sales@arcadiapublishing.com
For customer service and orders:
Toll-Free 1-888-313-2665

Visit us on the Internet at www.arcadiapublishing.com

*This book is dedicated to Maynard Harding, who did much to preserve the history of Parsons, and to those individuals who now protect Parsons's past and promote its future.*

# CONTENTS

# ACKNOWLEDGMENTS

This book would not have been possible without the support of the board of directors of the Iron Horse Historical Museum and the board of directors of the Parsons Historical Society Museum. Both groups greeted the project enthusiastically and made their extensive collections of photographs available. Unless otherwise indicated, all images are courtesy of the Iron Horse Historical Museum and the Parsons Historical Society Museum.

The authors also gratefully acknowledge two previously published works, Maynard Harding's *The Katy Railroad & Parsons, Kansas: A Chronology*, and *The Centennial Story of Parsons, Kansas: One Hundred Years of Progress*. Both volumes were valuable resources that helped make this volume a reality.

We also wish to thank those in the community who lent their support to this venture and to those who loaned us photographs, provided background material, reviewed the text, or provided technical assistance.

Most importantly, we thank our friends and families who have given of their time and who have provided steadfast encouragement throughout this adventure.

# INTRODUCTION

Parsons has always been a railroad town. Although the economy is now more diverse than it was in 1945 when the Missouri-Kansas-Texas Railroad, better known as the Katy, employed over 2,000 of its 18,000 citizens, Parsons remains deeply rooted in its railroad heritage. Katy Days, by far the largest of several annual citywide celebrations, brings railroad and history buffs to town. The Iron Horse Historical Museum, along with the Parsons Historical Society Museum, actively promotes the golden age of the Katy, and almost everyone in town knows someone who once worked for the railroad.

On any given day, 25 to 35 Union Pacific Railroad trains now make their way to Parsons, gliding into town after slowing along the section of track that makes a long, graceful curve north of town. They cross the primary east–west arteries of the community—Crawford Avenue, Main Street, Corning Avenue, and Appleton Avenue. Thanks to underpasses on Main Street and Corning Avenue, few motorists or pedestrians note their passage; these trains move with little fanfare, slipping out of town south toward Oklahoma.

However, 140 years ago it was very much a different story. In fact, at that time, there was a lot of interest in a train to Oklahoma, and that interest was shared by some very influential men.

The story of Parsons begins in 1868 in Emporia. Early in October of that year, a stagecoach brought a group of eastern investors to town. Among them were Judge Levi Parsons, president of the Land Grant Railroad and Trust Company, and Robert Smith Stevens, soon to be general construction manager for the Union Pacific Southern Branch Railroad. By the end of the meeting in Emporia, the group, led by Parsons, had acquired financial control of the Union Pacific Southern Branch, and he began to make plans for a railroad line south from Junction City through the Neosho River valley in southeast Kansas, across Oklahoma Territory, and finally on to the Gulf of Mexico. A proposed second line from Sedalia, Missouri, was planned to connect with the Union Pacific Southern Branch line.

While several other groups vied for the exclusive rights to build through the relative wilderness that was Oklahoma Territory, all were motivated by the government's promise to grant alternate sections of land along the route to the company that first reached the southern border of Kansas and provided the military with the rail line it wanted south from Fort Leavenworth. J. P. Morgan, Levi P. Morton, John D. Rockefeller, and George Denison, all of whom were just beginning their storied financial careers, backed the venture. Within five years, thanks in part to Stevens, the man who was the acknowledged motivating spirit of the company, it was the Katy enterprise that won the race and reached the Kansas border south of Chetopa on June 6, 1870. Within hours, the first passenger train made its way across Labette County and into Oklahoma Territory.

Within three months, the Parsons Town Company was formed. By November 1870, Stevens had purchased over 2,000 acres of land, and he, along with civil engineer L. F. Olney, planned the town, naming it for the president of the company and naming many streets for investors and railroad directors, including Crawford, Belmont, Morgan, Johnson, and Morton Avenues.

The same frenetic energy that brought the railroad to southeast Kansas seemed to instill a sense of optimism and faith in the future of the newly created community, and events justified that faith. Milton J. Reynolds, cofounder of the *Parsons Sun*, captured the spirit of the times when he proclaimed Parsons "the Infant Wonder of the West." Within a few years of its founding, the city had four newspapers, hundreds of homes, and a railroad complex, the focus of which was the Missouri-Kansas-Texas roundhouse, the most substantial building west of the Mississippi River. Thanks to the easy access the railroad provided, settlers poured into the area, and the population swelled. When the city was incorporated in 1871, there were several hundred citizens already living on the site. Eleven years later, the population was near 6,000.

In 1881, a group of prominent citizens formed the Forest Park Association, establishing 18 acres of parkland on the southeast edge of the city. Many of those individuals purchased another 46 acres east of Labette Creek to be used as fairgrounds and a riding area. By the 1890s, the town boasted a public library, a grand opera house, and a progressive educational system—indeed, all the trappings of a bona fide city, albeit a small one by eastern standards. By 1900, the citizens of Parsons were justifiably proud of their city; view books published in 1905 and 1908 epitomized that pride by naming Parsons the "Queen City of the Great Southwest." In 25 years, the infant wonder had matured and gained a crown.

Although dozens of cities across the country adopted similar titles for their municipalities, a strong case can be made that the title of queen city was more than civic hyperbole. The rough-and-tumble frontier days when there were an estimated 20 saloons in Parsons were over. Gone too were most of the wooden facade structures that had lined Main Street and Broadway Avenue. Multistoried brick buildings, some of which survive today, had replaced them. The small shacks that settlers first brought to town in addition to those they later constructed on-site were replaced by substantial working-class homes and a large number of elegant residences along what became known as "Silk Stocking Row," Morgan Avenue. Most impressive of all was the newest incarnation of the railroad's influence, the depot built in 1895. Complete with a clock tower that could be seen from almost any part of town, the Victorian-styled brick and stone structure had steam heat and private parlors for women travelers. Its location, at the end of Forrest Avenue (later known as Broadway Avenue), gave it a commanding presence in town, and the massive building dominated the skyline. Within 10 years, the facility was serving 30 passenger trains a day.

Besides providing revenue to the railroad, passengers were instrumental in the growth of Parsons in another way. Because the Katy line served those traveling from Chicago and St. Louis to points south through Texas and on to California, the city received a tremendous amount of word-of-mouth publicity. People who were visiting relatives and those who spent only a few minutes in the station waiting for their next train bought pieces of souvenir china and postcards. Handwritten notes on postcards often mentioned how well appointed and pretty Parsons seemed to those who saw it for the first time. Businesses such as International Harvester, the Baldwin Shirt Company, and Strasburger's Department Store fueled the local economy, along with the Queen City Creamery, the Parsons Bottle Works, the Knauer Cigar Factory, and hotels like the Mecca and the Matthewson House. Although the Katy Railroad was by far the largest employer, the presence of the Parsons State Hospital and, later, the Kansas Ordnance Plant, Hallmark, and the Coca-Cola Bottling Plant, along with the St. Louis and San Francisco (Frisco) Railroad, created a diverse and thriving business and service community.

America's entry into World War I placed a renewed dependency on the nation's transportation system, especially the rail lines. A total of 1,442 Parsons and Labette County residents served in the war; 61 were killed. Between 1917 and 1919, over 100,000 troops, including sick and wounded servicemen, traveled through Parsons. To meet the needs of the men, the railroad donated land between the new passenger station and the general office building for a canteen sponsored by the newly founded Labette County Chapter of the American Red Cross.

As it was in most of the nation, the 1920s was a time of general prosperity, although labor relations on the Katy came to a head early in the decade. For the second time in its history, the first being in 1886, the city was placed under martial law and the responsibility for the county government was delegated to the state when a general railroad strike began on July 8, 1922. Over 300 National Guardsmen were bivouacked at the Katy Athletic Field for the duration of the strike, which began as a pay-scale dispute. Before it was over, military forces had also assumed responsibility for the work of the city police department.

Of course, the decade brought more positive, permanent changes as well. The railroad opened the Katy Employees Hospital and the Katy Golf Course, the public school system expanded to form Parsons Junior College, and a new high school and junior college building took the place of the existing high school, which was built in 1893. When it was completed, the new facility was among the largest in Kansas.

While southeast Kansas was spared the sky-darkening dust storms of the 1930s that hit western and central Kansas, residents of Depression-era Parsons did contend with record-breaking heat and a general economic slowdown. But, because railroad employees' benefits were often federally regulated and business remained strong on the line, a Katy job was a good thing to have during the 1930s. And, in 1935, 1,625 Parsons residents were Katy employees. Thanks to rail passes for railroad employees and their families, a surprising number of residents traveled, at least regionally, during that time, and some even made their way to Chicago in 1933 to view the world's fair, a Century of Progress International Exposition. While individual residents may have had more woeful tales of the Depression, the city continued to promote itself as the center of commerce in southeast Kansas. An airmail envelope mailed during National Air Mail Week in 1938 sported a picture of the Parsons Post Office and the words "Parsons: Heart of the Southeast Kansas Industrial District."

By that time, Parsons could also claim a long list of people who had made their mark locally, nationally, and internationally. Two Kansas governors, Clyde Reed Sr. and Payne Ratner, called Parsons home. Walter Davidson, a Katy machinist, resigned his job in 1903 and moved to Milwaukee where he joined his brothers in the manufacture of motorcycles. Paul Hibbs, an office supply repairman, became a local celebrity in 1930 when he built the first airplane in Parsons, a detachable winged model nicknamed "the Doodlebug." George Pepperdine, the founder of Western Auto and Pepperdine University, spent his childhood in the Parsons area and was a graduate of Parsons Business College.

The 1940s brought both World War II and the Kansas Ordnance Plant to Parsons. While many of the plant employees were drawn from a five-county area in Kansas and from northeast Oklahoma and southwest Missouri, at its peak of operation, the plant employed 28,000. To accommodate the flood of workers, larger, older homes were subdivided into three or four apartments, and living quarters were constructed above garages, in basements, and in attics.

For Parsons, the last half of the 20th century was as remarkable as the second half of the 19th century. The general decline of the passenger railway system and changing shopping patterns across the country meant changes in Parsons as well. It was a blow to the city when the Katy Railroad moved its general offices to Denison, Texas, in 1957; over the next several years, 1,000 Katy jobs disappeared. By the late 1960s, when parts of downtown began to look a bit worn, the city turned to a federally funded urban renewal project, which was designed to revitalize the business district. Planned as a pedestrian mall and mostly completed by 1975, the project was a bold, progressive move on the part of the city, one in keeping with its adventuresome spirit.

Although the almost five-year project did remove many derelict buildings and provided updates on vital elements of the city's infrastructure, it also changed the face of Parsons, and several historic structures, foremost among them the Katy station, were lost. For almost 30 years, the Parsons Plaza was a fixture of downtown, but many of the structures associated with the plaza were damaged or destroyed by a tornado on April 19, 2000.

Parsons can be proud of its past and even more proud of its present. It has a strong sense of community, and because of the Union Pacific Railroad and the city's location on Route 400, a major east–west route across Kansas, it remains a regional transportation hub. Thanks to a local beautification committee, those early tourists who once wrote home about "pretty Parsons" would not be disappointed if they were to see the city today. Community volunteers and hardworking city officials ensure that the vision provided by railroad pioneer Stevens remains strong and that Parsons-on-the-Prairie continues to be what it has always been—a dynamic Kansas community.

# One

# FRONTIER DAYS

Very much the frontier town, Parsons was no more than two years old when this picture was taken, probably in 1873. It depicts Main Street looking west from the corner of Main Street and Central Avenue, now the Commercial Bank corner. Buildings include the United States Hotel, the Chicago Store, and the Sipple Brothers Grocery, the first grocery store in Parsons.

If guests of the Belmont House tired of the billiards room or the saloon, they had the luxury of retiring to a large gallery that overlooked one of the busiest streets in town. Built in 1871 by E. B. Stevens and U. L .C. Beard and located on the north side of Broadway Avenue, the Belmont House was the first hotel constructed in Parsons. The Katy Records building later stood at this location.

Central and Broadway Avenues are the scene of this early Parsons picture. The land offices and boot and shoe shop are on Central Avenue; the hardware store is at 1830 Broadway. The drugstore across the street from the hardware store on the corner was the first in town, opened by Dr. T. L. Warren, who was also one of the first physicians.

Based on the number of horses that are tethered in front of the establishment, the dry goods store of G. W. Everhart seems a prosperous place, despite the competition from similar nearby stores that advertised cheaper goods. Everhart's store was located on the northeast corner of Main Street and Central Avenue. Later the Kimball Hotel was built on this site. The Settlers Store was established in 1871 by M. Johnson.

Built as the St. James Hotel, this three-story brick structure was hailed by local newspaper reporters as the finest building in Parsons. Ground was broken on June 8, 1872, on the northwest corner of Central Avenue and Broadway Avenue, then known as Riggs and Forrest Avenues. The hotel contained 22 rooms and was 50 feet square. The building later became the Red Cross Drug Store.

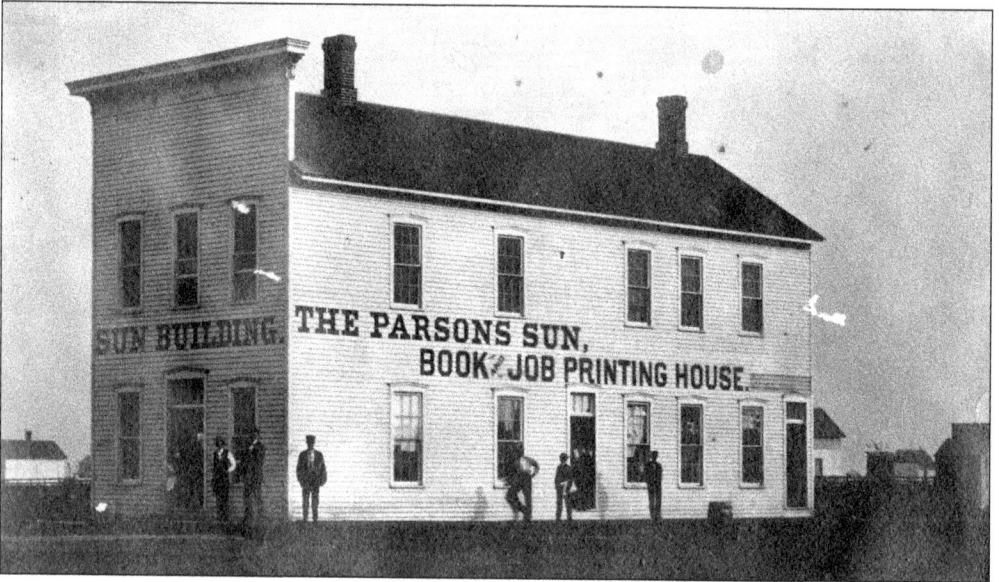

The *Parsons Sun* began publication on June 17, 1871, only two months after the city government was organized. The first home of the newspaper was located on the corner of Central Avenue and Belmont Avenue and was built by W. G. Melville. Milton W. Reynolds, known as "Kickin' Bird" Reynolds, along with Leslie J. Perry, published the newspaper. It was Reynolds who first dubbed Parsons "the Infant Wonder of the West." The St. Louis and San Francisco (Frisco) Railroad station was later constructed on this site, now occupied by Belmont Towers.

Footpaths zigzag their way to downtown Parsons in this photograph, which was probably taken before 1875. It depicts the city's two primary streets. To the left is Forrest Avenue (Broadway Avenue), and to the right is Johnson Avenue (Main Street). This view looks west from the location later occupied by Parsons City Hall and the Parsons Municipal Building.

14

Bobcat seem to be in plentiful supply, based on this interior shot of W. H. DeJarnette's business, which was located at 1814–1816 Washington Avenue. DeJarnette owned and operated the business for many years. This photograph was probably taken in an adjacent storage shed; the business was housed in a brick building that remained standing well into the 20th century.

The new depot of the Missouri-Kansas-Texas Railroad, also known as the Katy Railroad, towers above the town in this photograph, which shows Broadway Avenue west from Eighteenth Street. The original depot was a frame structure; the brick one shown here was advertised by local officials as the best depot in the state of Kansas. The three-story brick building on the north side of the street was the St. James Hotel.

All paths lead to the Katy station in this photograph taken shortly after its completion. Even though the Missouri-Kansas-Texas Railroad soon outgrew this structure and built an even larger and more elaborate depot in 1895, this building was the pride of Parsons when it was opened to the public on March 2, 1872. The depot cost $20,000 and was built of brick and stone.

This faded photograph captures an important event in early Katy history. Work began on the Katy roundhouse in October 1871. This photograph was probably taken the next year as the walls of the roundhouse neared completion. Made of blue limestone quarried at Burlington with additional limestone from a quarry in Council Grove, the roundhouse cost $300,000.

Every doorway is full of employees at the Parsons Mills. Originally located in Americus, the business was moved to Parsons and owned by Angell Matthewson, L. S. Hamilton, and G. W. Chess. The flour mill was located at Twenty-first Street and Washington Avenue and operated until 1877.

The south side of the 1800 block of Broadway Avenue housed a variety of businesses, as this early downtown photograph attests. Included are the City Bakery, the Current and Cook Dry Goods Store, the City Shoe Store, the W. C. Holmes Drug Store, and the store of merchant-tailor B. Gormley. Pedestrians no doubt used the planked sidewalk in front of the hardware store to cross often muddy streets.

This photograph captures an outing of the Parsons Rifle Team of 1886–1887. While the prairie offered lots of wild game and wide-open spaces, dress for the occasion was more formal than modern game hunting requires. The men wore hats and ties, and the women wore large, ornate hats. However, to modern-day viewers, only the dog seems appropriately dressed.

While several early photographs of Parsons show a crowded business district, in this photograph, merchants' signs and a lone wagon dominate the streetscape. The view looks west on Main Street from Eighteenth Street. Businesses include the City Meat Market; Brown, Brinton and Company; and the Settlers Store.

The Hobson Normal Institute, located at Twenty-fourth Street and Gandy Avenue, later Grand Avenue, opened in 1882 and operated for approximately 10 years. A forerunner of Douglas School, the institute served African American students in a two-story wooden structure. It was established with an initial private donation of $1,000. This rare photograph shows students before school or during recess under the watchful eyes of a bearded gentleman.

The rural surroundings of this 1885 photograph are misleading. At first glance, it appears to show a farm or a small settlement. Instead, the scene is the 1900 block of Washington Avenue not far from the busy downtown area around the Katy station.

The studio-printed caption on this photograph sums up the scene pretty well: "A busy day on Central Avenue in Parsons, Kansas." Although they were surprisingly wide, wooden sidewalks were still a part of downtown in 1885 when this photograph was taken. The view looks north on Central Avenue before the water tower or St. Patrick's Catholic Church were constructed.

Traffic, both pedestrian and carriage, was heavy on the southeast corner of Johnson Avenue and Central Avenue when this May 1886 photograph was taken. Although not all these people were on their way to the McKim and Reeme Drug Store, the business did seem to sell an extraordinarily wide variety of items, including Sherwin-Williams paint. Later this establishment was known as the Fees Brothers Drug Store.

# Two

# AROUND TOWN

Traffic was sparse on Broadway Avenue when this 1920s photograph was taken. The view is east from Central Avenue. The Parsons Business College occupied the three-story building on the southeast corner of the intersection. The college operated for 61 years in Parsons. For many of those years, it was under the direction of Prof. J .C. Olson.

The American Express Company served the Parsons area from the late 1890s until the early 1920s. The office was first located at Twentieth Street and Forrest Avenue and later at 1930 Main Street. This photograph from about 1900 captures two uniformed company employees on a residential street.

Water, probably from a recent storm, filled Central Avenue when amateur photographer C. E. Cadmus took this photograph, which captures parts of three Parsons landmarks from the dawn of the 20th century. The building in the center of the photograph was the Frisco depot. The domed corner of the Matthewson Hotel is visible behind it, and the familiar silhouette of the Katy station clock tower is on the far left-hand side of the photograph. The view looks north down Central Avenue. While Cadmus was not associated with any of the studios in town, the images he captured are among the best of early-day Parsons.

This photograph looks east from Central Avenue and Main Street, showing both the north and south sides of Main Street. The tall building in the distance on the left-hand side was Strasburger's Department Store. While business in general seemed to be booming, one store owner was calling it quits. The banner outside the store on the right-hand side of the photograph reads, "Entire Stock to Be Sold at Auction."

St. Patrick's Catholic Church looks much the same today as it did when trees lined Central Avenue. The church, which was under construction for nearly nine years from 1891 until 1900, is located at Stevens and Central Avenues. Since its completion, the Romanesque-style brick and stone church has been one of the most prominent structures in Parsons.

For many years, the Elks Theatre and the Parsons Business College were two of the most distinctive and impressive structures in Parsons. This photograph captures a band as it parades down Eighteenth Street. The view looks to the south across Broadway Avenue. While the exact occasion of the celebration is not known, the flag and the red, white, and blue bunting on the front of the Elks building indicate a patriotic event.

The White building was one of largest downtown business structures in Parsons around 1900. Located on the northeast corner of Eighteenth Street and Main Street, it later became Strasburger's Department Store. The store was destroyed by fire, and a new Strasburger building, one that stands today on the same location, took its place.

Harriet Beecher Stowe's famed abolitionist novel came to the screen in 1927, complete with heart-tugging sentiment. It was a big hit nationwide. The film was shown at the Best Theatre in the fall of 1928, and, judging by the promotional fanfare it received, it lost none of its appeal to pretalkie audiences. The Best was located at 1819–1821 Main Street.

Before it became a sports complex—with football, baseball, and softball fields—the Marvel Park area was a fairgrounds and a place for a variety of sporting events. This rare photograph, probably taken in the 1920s, shows a surrey race on the oval track as a large crowd watches.

Before the automobile show era, locals got their first views of the newest models of cars the old-fashioned way, by going to the dealership. This Peterson Studio photograph shows new Fords arriving at the W. N. Chapman Agency at 1625 Main Street. The domed roof and columned front of the First Baptist Church are in the background.

When this C. E. Cadmus photograph was taken, the area east of Labette Creek was countryside. Because traffic was light, motorists had the luxury of stopping their vehicles to take in the view. The original caption notes that the photograph was taken shortly after the two-lane concrete bridge was completed.

While it is sometimes difficult to get a real sense of an area with only a snapshot as a reference, this view of the south side of the 1900 block of Main Street seems to capture the spirit of the place. It looks west toward the subway and the Missouri-Kansas-Texas Railroad tracks. Nusbaum's Cash Department Store, "the Store that Saves You Money," along with the John Scaletty Metal Works and Blake's Furniture were the businesses on the east half of the block.

For many years, the subway that linked east and west Main Street was a single lane, heavily fenced to prevent pedestrians from interfering with interurban traffic. This rare Peterson Studio photograph shows the south side of the 1900 block of Main Street. The corner building was the St. Clair Hotel. Faded signage on the building advertises lodging for 25¢.

This photograph captures the view at approximately Twentieth and Main Streets, the west entrance to the subway. On the north side of the street is the Curtis Hotel. The crude frame structure on the south side of Main Street is a defunct short-order café that had visions of grandeur, called the King of Chili.

The owner of the tailor shop on the south side of the 1900 block of Main Street has clearly taken advantage of Charlie Chaplin's popularity in film to promote the business. The life-size, freestanding figure bears a striking resemblance to Chaplin's the Little Tramp. It reminds passersby that the shop not only offers suits made to order but also offers shirts pressed "while you wait."

Motorcycle racing was another popular sport held at Marvel Park. This photograph was taken before the area around the track was fenced. Despite the fact that the early-day motorcycles look more like motorized bicycles, townspeople are out in force to see the event. One couple enjoys the view from the comforts of their horse-drawn carriage.

The interurban tracks are clearly visible in this 1920s view of Main Street taken from Central Avenue looking east. The interurban service began in 1912, with Parsons as the northernmost terminal. The line stretched as far south as Nowata, Oklahoma, with stops in Cherryvale, Independence, and Coffeyville. The Bing Clothing Store, Holmes Drug, and Woolworth's stand out in this cityscape. A close examination of the photograph reveals that several doctors and dentists had offices on this block, including a Dr. Cockrell, who advertised a "no pain dental service."

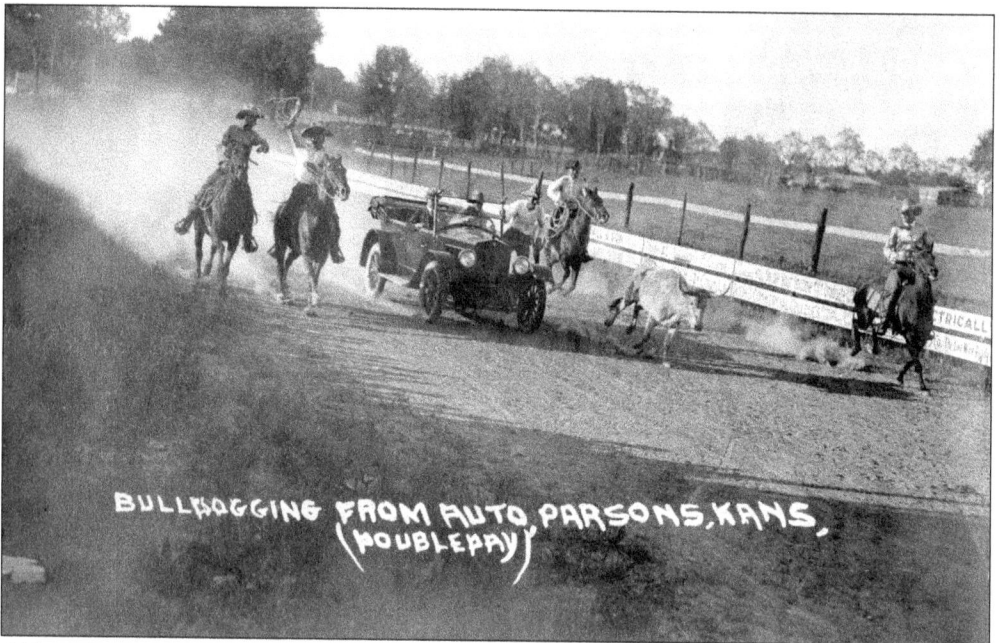

BULLDOGGING FROM AUTO, PARSONS, KANS.
(DOUBLEPAY)

Although it certainly took skill, there does not seem to be much sport involved in this odd combination of automobile racing and rodeo. The original caption on this photograph reads, "Bulldogging from Auto, Parsons, Kans." The scene is the oval track at Marvel Park just east of Labette Creek. The signs on the fence are advertisements, including one for Olson's Business College.

Parson, Kansas, Septiembre de 1928

Club Billiards, the former First National Bank building, is the backdrop for this photograph of the Katy Reclaim Mexican Band, taken in September 1928. Workers migrated from Mexico to claim railroad jobs, and an active Hispanic community remains in Parsons. This photograph was taken on the southwest corner of Central Avenue and Broadway Avenue, home to Parsons's first bank. (Courtesy of Tony Munoz.)

Originally built in the 1920s as a private hospital by Dr. Julius Rotter, the Parsons Old Ladies Home was located at 1607 Main Street. It was home to many senior citizens from the mid-1930s until the late 1970s. At that time, the building was sold to the First Baptist Church. The Parsons Old Ladies Home was razed in 1980.

Edith Hinthorn owned and operated the Parsons Hospital and Maternity Home, which was located at 1403 Main Street. While the city had two other hospitals by the mid-1920s, Mercy Hospital and the Katy Hospital, many expectant mothers chose this less institutional alternative. Until the 1960s, houses lined most of Main Street east of Sixteenth Street.

This 1930s downtown window display promotes the YMCA's annual subscription drive during the month of October. The goal was to raise $5,000. For many years, the YMCA played an important role in the social life of Parsons's youth. As one of the posters exclaims, "Here the Boy Is King!"

The original of this extraordinary photograph was hand colored in soft hues of blue, green, yellow, and pink. Even though the children's 19th-century-style costumes were probably homemade, they seem opulent by Depression-era standards. The children pose on the front lawn of the McKinley School building, constructed in 1912. This photograph dates from the early 1930s.

Although its location remains a mystery, this hot dog stand must have been one of the smallest eateries ever in Parsons. However, while the owners may have scrimped on the building itself, they splurged on the sign. When lit, the neon lined, wiener-shaped dog had a wagging tail. The photograph was probably taken in the 1930s.

The world's tallest man visited Parsons in the late 1930s. Robert Pershing Wadlow was born in 1918 in Alston, Illinois. By the time he was 20 years old, he was 8 feet 11 inches tall and a national celebrity. As a spokesperson for a well-known shoe company, Wadlow, who was reported to wear a size 37 AA shoe, made an appearance at Smith's Shoe Store on Main Street. He is the man in the light shirt and tie with his head down. One of Wadlow's shoes, used as a promotional item on the tour, is housed in the Iron Horse Historical Museum in Parsons.

Four of Parsons's five theaters are visible in this late-1940s view of Main Street. Taken from the Katy overpass looking east, the theaters are the Katy, the Parsons, the Uptown, and the Kansan. Barnes Perdue managed all four theaters. The fifth theater operating at the time was the appropriately named West Theatre, located west of the subway.

Decked out in their best farmhand duds, employees of the Parsons Theatre pose in front of an advertisement for the current feature, *Wild Harvest*. Despite their festive sashes and the presence of Allan Ladd, Dorothy Lamour, and Robert Preston in the film, by all accounts, the 1947 production was not as successful as this portrait is memorable.

This Leon Crooks Studio photograph captures Broadway Avenue during the Christmas season. Taken from the 1700 block, it looks west to the Katy station. Businesses on the left-hand side of the street, the south side, include Esther's Beauty Service, Sears, the Individual Mausoleum Company, Martin's Furniture, and the Faye Hotel.

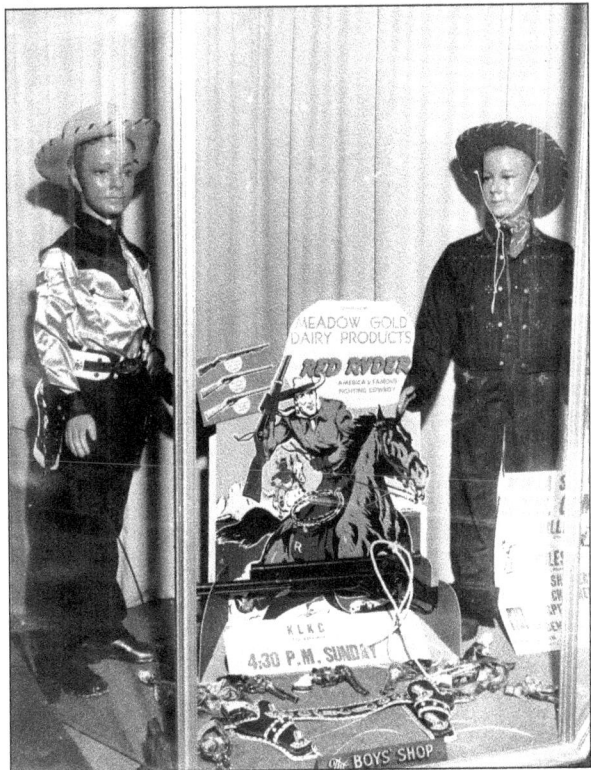

Westerns were one of the most popular entertainment genres in the late 1940s and 1950s. Whether it was a wide-screen movie, a weekly television show, or a radio program, audiences could not get enough of the Old West. This display window promotes the *Red Ryder* radio show, which ran from 1942 until the early 1950s. It could be heard on KLKC Radio, Parsons's only radio station "at the top o' the dial."

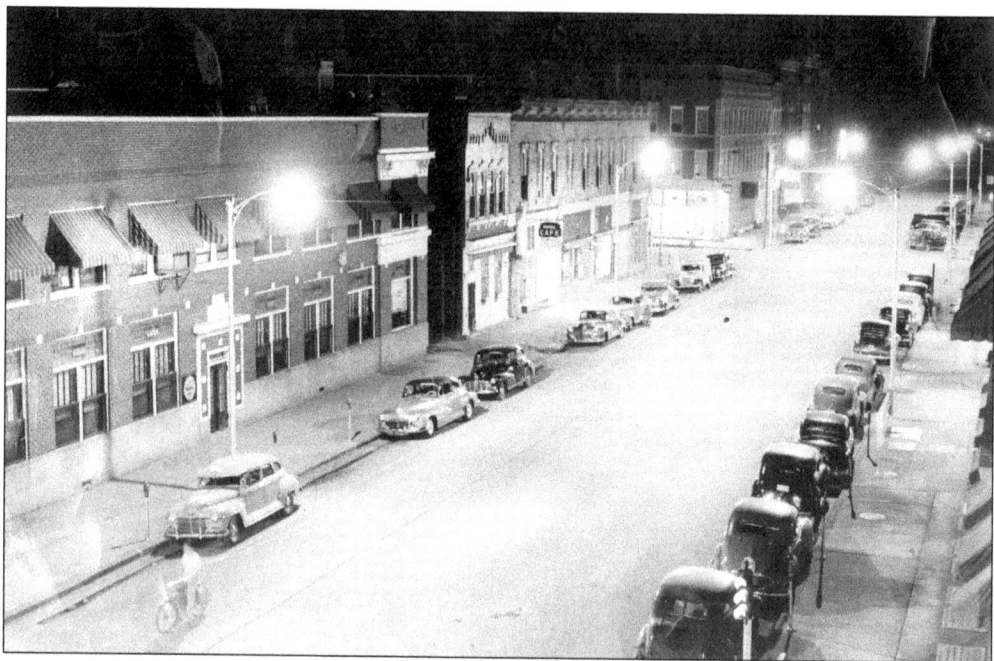

This atmospheric night view of Central Avenue and Main Street looking south was probably taken from the second floor or the roof of the Commercial Bank. The old State Bank building with awnings is on the left-hand side of the view, along with the Royal Café.

The Parsons Carnegie Library opened in the spring of 1909. It had been in use for over 40 years when this story hour photograph was taken in the early 1950s. Charles Nordyke reads to young patrons in the junior library, located in the basement. The portrait of Andrew Carnegie still hangs in the facility, which is now the Carnegie Arts Center. (Courtesy of the Parsons Public Library.)

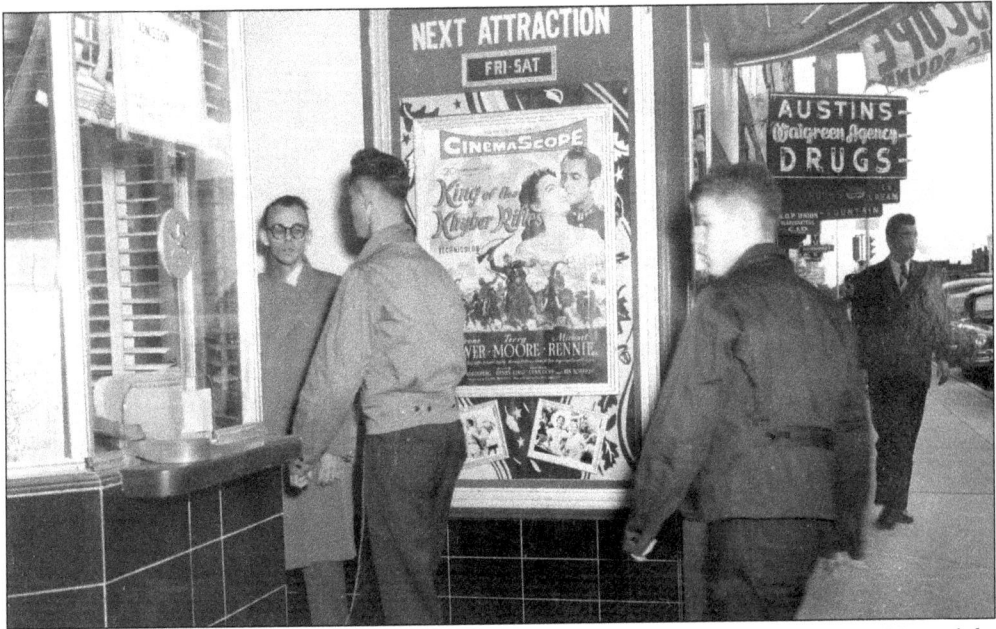

At the time this photograph was taken, the big draw at the Parsons Theatre was *King of the Khyber Rifles*, which was released in 1953 and starred Tyrone Power and Terry Moore. Although it was made in Cinemascope, the film was often shown on standard-size screens like the one in this theater. Prices for evening and weekend shows were 65¢ for adults, 45¢ for students, and 25¢ for children. Matinee prices were slightly lower.

Carl Hunter's Dari-Delite was located at 3128 Main Street. It often sponsored attention-getting promotions, such as sock hops that showcased live bands. This early-1960s photograph illustrates another pop culture tie-in, the Purple People Eater Sundae. As the hand-painted sign says, "You Eat It Before It Eats You!"

This rare nighttime view shows the glow of the West Theatre marquee. The photograph was taken from Twenty-second and Main Streets looking east. The presence of the interurban trolley tracks dates the photograph before 1952, when the last of the tracks were removed. Wilcox Standard Gasoline was located at 2131 Main Street.

Although several homes are under construction, when this photograph was taken, the Eastborough housing addition consisted of 10 residences. Telephone poles line Main Street, in what was then the easternmost part of town. As originally platted, Parsons was small, only 11.5 blocks north and south and 8 blocks east and west. Even though it expanded at a steady pace, maps as late as 1912 show undeveloped land west of Twenty-sixth Street and east of Labette Creek.

# *Three*

# BUSINESS AS USUAL

Before the horseless carriage made an appearance in Parsons, dozens of businesses centered on the care and boarding of horses. Before 1900, most of the livery stables were located east of Seventeenth Street on Washington Avenue and on Main Street. This early photograph shows the Blair and Malott blacksmith shop. Two of the men are wearing blacksmith aprons.

The Hoke Brothers Ice Plant operated for approximately 15 years, from 1890 through the second decade of the 20th century. This Peterson Studio photograph shows the plant and the fleet of wagons that delivered ice to businesses and residents on a daily basis. The deliverymen wear what appears to be the standard uniform for Hoke employees—white pants, shirt, and hat. The plant was located on the 2000 block of Gabriel Avenue.

There was no frozen food section or deli; however, Donaldson Grocery, which was located at 610 North Twenty-sixth Street, did have plenty of fresh fruit and canned goods. In addition, the store owner seemed to have a knack for displaying items. A stalk of bananas, a selection of brooms, and a large Heinz pickle-shaped sign hang from the ceiling.

While fresh oysters now have to be purchased out of town or have to be specially ordered, they were received daily by express at O. L. Evans Groceries when this photograph was taken around 1908. Located at 1810 Main Street, the store advertises cornflakes, dill pickles, and Heinz Sauer Kraut. Fresh produce in baskets also grace the display windows.

Employees of the Kress store gather for a formal portrait in 1909. The Kress five-and-dime operated in Parsons for 70 years from 1907 until 1977. The original store was a victim of the November 13, 1907, fire, and this photograph, in all likelihood, commemorated the opening of the rebuilt store.

The International Harvester Supply Office, located west of the YMCA building, is the subject of this C. E. Cadmus photograph. While the work area seems cramped and primitive by today's standards, it was no doubt considered a well-appointed space when this photograph was taken. The young typist's hairdo and the tall, removable shirt collar of the man operating the press were typical of pre–World War I office attire. The 1912 calendar on the wall was courtesy of the First National Bank of Parsons.

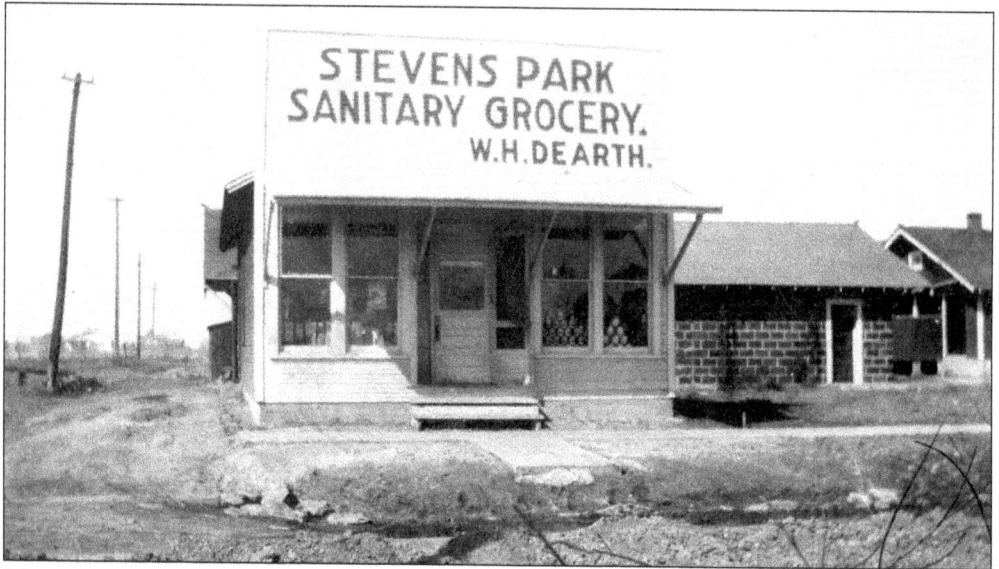

The supermarket was a post–World War II phenomenon. Before then, most people bought groceries from neighborhood markets that where scattered throughout the community within easy walking distance of their homes. W. H. Dearth was proprietor of one such market, the Stevens Park Sanitary Grocery. The Stevens addition encompasses the area from Thirtieth Street to Thirty-second Street and from Main Street to Gabriel Avenue, an area that includes the Katy Hospital. None of the local markets remain in business, but several buildings that once housed them still stand in the city.

Holiday hoopla is nothing new as this early-1900s photograph illustrates. L. W. Waits poses for an Electric Studio portrait as Santa. He wears a long fur coat and prepares to haul a hodgepodge of gifts from the White Furniture Company. The store was first located at 1801 Main Street and later moved to 1707 Main Street. It closed in 1952 after 64 years of operation.

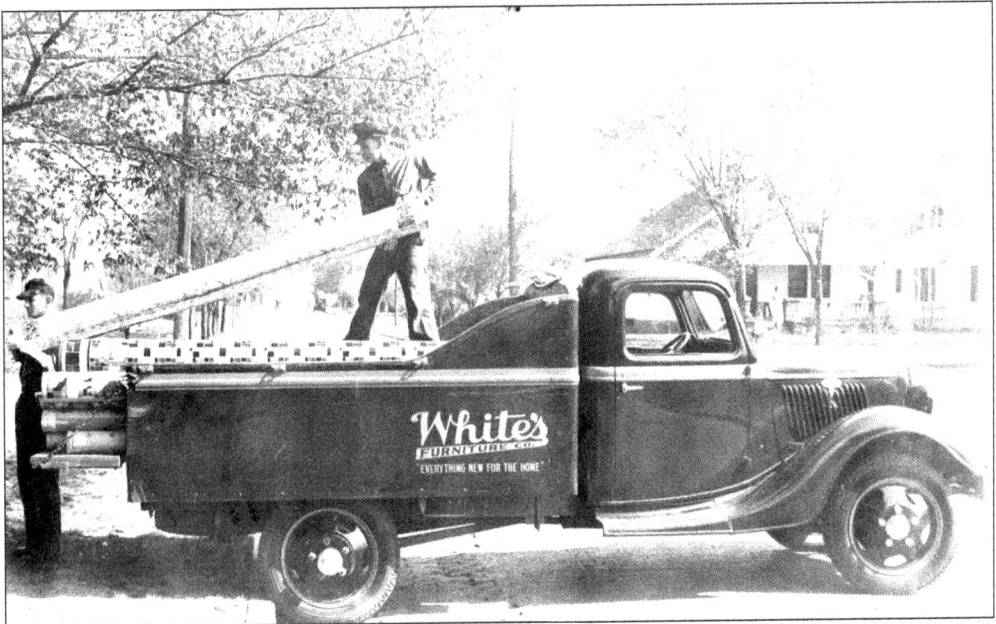

Decades later, White's continued its delivery service. Uniformed employee Glen Smith brings a stylish rug and a roll of linoleum to a home on Twenty-seventh Street. Neighbors across the way watch with interest in this 1936 photograph. Today homes in the neighborhood remain much the same as they were at that time.

The East Side Market was located in the 200 block of North Central Avenue. While its proprietor, R. J. O'Brien, clearly specialized in meat and groceries, this 1924 window display hoped to lure female customers with its emphasis on bubble and olive oil soap and its illustrations of young women with peaches-and-cream complexions.

T-bone steaks were 30¢ a pound, and pork chops were 25¢ a pound when this interior view of the East Side Market was taken in 1924. The poster on the back wall advertises Armour's Star Hams. Besides a variety of meats, the East Side Market also sold pickles, including sour, sweet, dill, or mixed.

The Parsons Commercial Bank was founded and chartered as Parsons Savings Bank on May 24, 1874; the bank changed its name to the Parsons Commercial Bank in August 1878. It was first located at 110 South Central Avenue but later moved to a facility on the corner of Central Avenue and Main Street, its present location. In August 1990, the bank was renamed the Commercial Bank.

The interior of the Parsons Commercial Bank was both beautiful and functional. While the light fixtures harken to an earlier era when the arts and crafts movement was in vogue around 1900, the sleek, stylized service island dates the photograph to the 1920s, when the art deco style was popular.

Parsons had several large buildings that were interesting architecturally; however, few smaller structures competed with the detail on the Parsons Building and Loan, located at 1909 Main Street. The arched door and stacked windows were unusual, but the stonework at the top of the building was its crowning glory.

The Main Street Cafeteria was typical of eateries in Parsons during the early part of the 20th century. Although Main Street was a through street, it was Broadway Avenue with its proximity to the Katy depot that was considered the primary business thoroughfare. On the day this photograph was taken, the cafeteria was promoting rainbow trout.

Robeson-Powell Drugs was the second of four drugstores in the same location at 1824 Main Street. Holmes Drug operated from 1912 until 1924, the Robeson-Powell was from 1925 to 1938, the Robeson Pharmacy was from 1938 to 1951, and Austin's Pharmacy was from 1951 to 1967. The ribbed glass tiles on the storefront were typical of businesses downtown. Several examples of the purplish-hued glass are still visible on Main Street.

The cloche hat and flapper-style dress in the window of the Fashion Shop date this photograph to the 1920s. Before World War I, most clothing was custom-made, but by the end of the war, shoppers bought "ready-to-wear, off-the-rack" clothing. The owner's attempt to display stylish merchandise is offset by the more practical window treatment in the plumber's shop next door.

Opening Day. March 18. 1939

The Brown Oil Company opened for business on March 18, 1939. Located on the southwest corner of Eighteenth Street and Belmont Avenue, the brick and stucco building had a distinct art moderne design, typical of pre–World War II service stations. A young man with his bicycle near the Mobilgas pumps found his way into this photograph, probably without the knowledge of those posing for the camera.

The Fawcett's Gift and China Shop celebrated its grand opening in 1945. The shop, located at 1812 Main Street, featured jewelry, leather goods, pottery, toys, silver, books, perfume, and a large selection of brick-a-brack. A close examination of the store's inventory identifies many future collectible pieces.

48

The remodeled Johnson's Café was the epitome of modern when this photograph was taken in 1936. The wall coverings, light fixtures, and ceiling tiles were strictly utilitarian, but the sleekly styled chairs, chrome-edged countertops, and geometric floor tile made the area functionally chic. The café was located at 110 North Central Avenue.

The Parsons Stockyards was a busy place when this photograph was taken in 1935. The parking lot is full of farm trucks, most of which have beds with wooden sides. Two gas pumps are located in front of the small building at center right. Although its location has changed, the stockyards continue to serve the area.

A handwritten notation on the back of this photograph identifies it as Louie's Drive In at 3128 Main Street. The location, near where the Frisco railroad tracks crossed Main Street, was probably a popular one. Although it was a self-service eatery, the prices were certainly right, and the two men who are posing underneath the drive-in's canopy look like they are ready to prepare another pizzaburger or chicken.

At one time, full-service gas stations were located on all four corners of the intersection at Sixteenth and Main Streets. The Texaco station was on the southwest corner. The rear of the Parsons Municipal Building is visible on the extreme right-hand side of the photograph behind the one-story house. The photograph is from about 1960. Before it was demolished, the service station was used as a storage facility.

50

# Four

# CELEBRATIONS

Crowds gather near the southwest corner of Seventeenth Street and Main Street to watch the circus as it makes its way across town. This photograph is one of at least seven photographs that document the event, which probably took place in 1911. Several young ladies can be seen taking advantage of the early construction materials on the site of the new Parsons Post Office. Even though they are seated, their perch afforded a good view of the ornate wagons as they passed city hall, which is obscured by the trees that once filled the block.

Members of the Parsons Fire Department pose for a parade picture in 1898. The horse-drawn wagon and ladder team is on Forrest Avenue where the department was located before it moved to Washington Avenue. The original firehouse was later torn down, and views of the site in 1916 show a vacant lot.

THE BEST LAUNDRY, IN THE BEST TOWN, IN THE BEST STATE & EMPLOYS THE BEST LOOKING GIRLS.

Although there is no record stating if it was voted best float in the parade, one thing is for sure: the makers of this Parsons State Hospital float knew how to promote themselves. The state legislature established the State Hospital for Epileptic Patients in 1899, but the first building did not open until 1903. This photograph is from about 1915. The hospital was renamed Parsons State Training School in 1957. It is now the Parsons State Hospital and Training Center.

Employees of the Katy shops were active in community events. They sponsored—and were members of—a variety of sports teams, and no Parsons parade was without at least one Katy-sponsored float. This elaborate entry dates from the 1890s and was sponsored by employees of the boiler shop. The men are dressed for the occasion, sporting dark shirts and white, hand-tied bows.

Even though the photograph that captured the moment is faded, it was a warm, sunny day when a crowd gathered to commemorate the laying of the cornerstone for the Parsons Post Office on July 3, 1912. The Parsons Carnegie Library next door was three years old when the post office construction began. The wood shack on the left-hand side of the photograph housed the construction office.

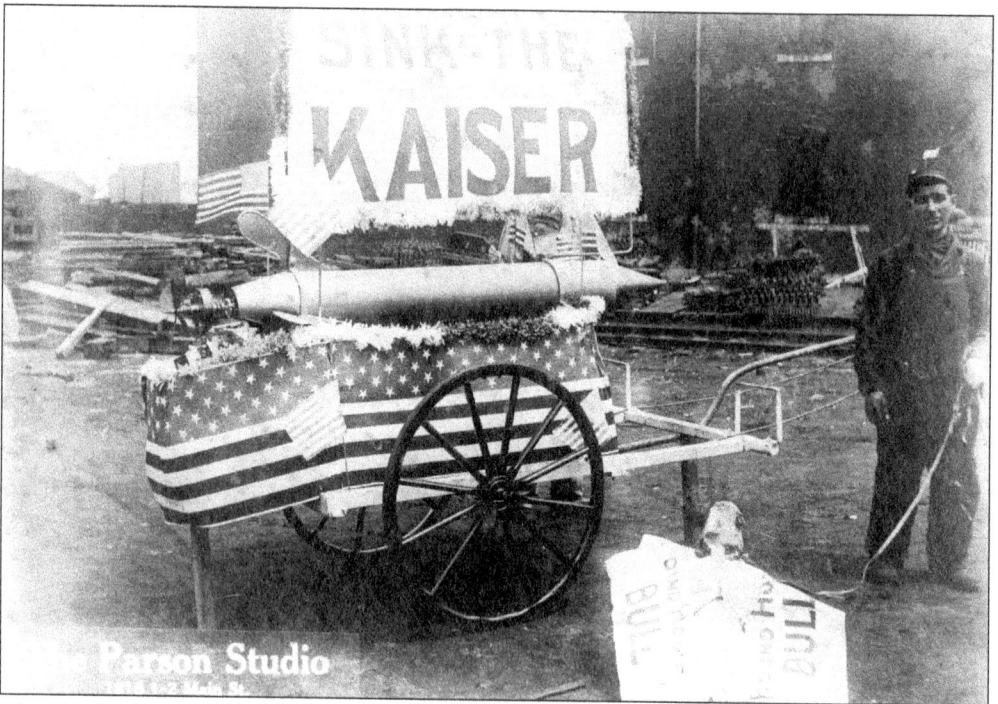

The Parson Studio, which was located at 1815½ Main Street, took this photograph of an entry in the Katy roundhouse parade. The United States entered World War I in April 1917, the same year that this photograph was taken. It is clear that anti-kaiser sentiment had swept the nation. Less clear to modern viewers is the crumpled signage containing the words "Round House Bull."

Although it looks like this patriotic float is decorated with flowers, the effect has been created with a more mundane material—shredded paper. Nevertheless, the float is striking, and its message is clear. This photograph was taken on July 4, 1916, nine months before the United States entered World War I.

The corner of Eighteenth Street and Broadway Avenue is the scene of Parsons's first dairy show, held in November 1917. According to the signage, visitors were treated to lectures, demonstrations, and a public livestock sale. The four-story original Strasburger building is visible in this view, which looks north. This photograph also captures a close-up view of the ornate globe light fixtures that once graced the business district.

It is hard to imagine the time it must have taken to decorate these two cars for the 1916 Fourth of July parade. Even those in the lead car are decorated head to toe. However, just as interesting to modern viewers is the parade's background, the post office box on the telephone pole, and the advertisements in the lot behind the car. These include the Parsons Motor Company, Sweetheart Flour, and Blue Valley Butter. This photograph was taken at the corner of Eighteenth Street and Broadway Avenue.

Flags line both sides of Main Street as a large crowd gathers downtown to watch the Rotary parade on April 7, 1924. The flag bearer leading the festivities turns north from Main Street onto Central Avenue. The ornate building with the shingled facade and the large, arched window is the Best Theatre, later renamed the Kansan.

While it is shamelessly commercial, there is no denying that this float is as stylish as the clothes worn by those associated with it. Lambert and Duffy were two of the leading clothiers in Parsons, and a store by that name operated for almost 90 years. The float in front of the boys promotes the Harris Packard dealership.

The Tri-State Fair was an annual event in Parsons during the 1920s. Held in the fall, it featured carnival rides, a rodeo, a parade, and a variety of exhibits. This photograph was taken during the 1921 fair, which was held from September 5 until September 10. If this float entry is any indication, the parade that year was an elaborate one. Even the horses pulling the float sport headdresses.

Children gather to watch circus wagons as they make their way across town. This C. E. Cadmus photograph was taken south of the Missouri-Kansas-Texas Railroad depot as a six-horse team approached the tracks, probably near Appleton Avenue. The circus was in town for one day, September 16. The front ornate wagon holds a zebra.

Although historic downtown Parsons has been the victim of multiple fires, a tornado, and general progress, the south side of the 1700 block of Main Street has remained intact. This photograph, taken as a crowd gathers to watch a parade, captures the essence of Main Street life. The scene dates from approximately 1911.

In one form or another, a YMCA float was a fixture of almost every parade in Parsons. This float features a young man in a large tub of water; his presence is meant to promote the swimming classes offered at the YMCA. The Parsons Carnegie Library, the Presbyterian church, and the Southwestern Bell Telephone building can be seen in this view of Seventeenth Street. Morris Studio took the photograph.

Kansans celebrated the state's centennial in a variety of ways in 1961. An astonishing array of souvenirs graced gift shops, cities minted their own centennial coins, and parades like this one made their way down main streets across the state. The photograph above shows Main Street as the parade travels west past the Parsons Theatre; it also provides a glimpse of the newly remodeled First National Bank. As a reminder of pioneer days, the Parsons centennial parade travels east to west along Main Street. The photograph below shows a horseless carriage as it passes Eighteenth Street. Newberry's, located in the former Steele Hardware building, is now Bleacher Gear.

A tie was definitely optional at the Missouri-Kansas-Texas Railroad apprentice picnic held on August 25, 1926. In fact, only a few men sport one and opt for what was probably considered business casual of the day. While this Morris Studio photograph was meant to commemorate the annual event, the extraordinary clarity of the image allows modern viewers the chance to

The Tri-State Fair was one of the largest annual celebrations in Parsons and was usually held at the Marvel Park fairgrounds. This Electric Studio photograph illustrates the wide range of activities available to fairgoers. Livestock competitions took place on part of the fairgrounds' oval track in front of the wooden grandstand. The elevated platform was used as a speaker's or

PICNIC AUG 25 1926

study the faces of the men who worked at the Katy while honing their various skills. In an age when the majority of photographs were formal portraits, it also provides a rare glimpse of 1920s informal recreational attire. Although the exact location of the event is unknown, it is probably Forest Park, which was as popular a gathering place then as it is now.

SEPT 5-10 1924

judge's box when musicians were not occupying it. The area north and east of the grandstand was home to an unusual spiral-shaped slide. To the south, various booths and a Ferris wheel created a carnival atmosphere not unlike the modern Labette County Fair.

61

The Parsons Plaza was meant to be the crowning jewel of the urban renewal project. When it was completed in the early 1970s, it seemed to epitomize the future of retail shopping that would take place in a people-friendly, urbane, parklike atmosphere, free from the worries of traffic. The view looks east from the 1800 block of Main Street.

The plaza was not yet complete when this Christmastime postcard was produced. The freestanding white structure, a miniature version of the gazebo, was home to a drinking fountain and a pay telephone. The large circles were planters. The brick serpentine wall was one of two that were features of the mall, with one at the east end and one at the west end. This photograph looks west from Seventeenth Street.

*Five*

# CIVIC PRIDE

Pedestrians who passed the southwest corner of Seventeenth and Main Streets on September 3, 1912, might have been surprised by the progress construction workers made on the new Parsons Post Office. However, they may not have been pleased that the stones used to form the columnlike decorations on the north and east sides of the structure were blocking the sidewalk. (Courtesy of the Parsons Post Office.)

Rural free delivery postal wagons gathered on Central Avenue for this photograph, which was taken on May 24, 1902. Each wagon displays the words "RFD U.S. Mail" and the number assigned to each unit. The building directly behind the last wagon on the corner is the First National Bank building. (Courtesy of the Parsons Post Office.)

H. F. Hall was Parsons fire chief when this photograph was taken in October 1897. Fire headquarters was located at 1815 Broadway Avenue. For many years, the wooden water tower was a fixture of downtown and a dominant part of the skyline. Its only nearby competition was the clock tower of the Katy station.

One of the earliest photographs of the Parsons Fire Department is this J. F. Standiford photograph, dated 1885. Members of Hose Company No. 2, along with two youngsters, pose in front of the original library building, located on the corner of Forrest Avenue and Eighteenth Street.

In 1882, the first graduate of Parsons High School received her diploma. That honor went to Maude G. Keyser, the sole graduate. By 1889, when this Parsons High School photograph was taken, more than a dozen graduates crossed the stage at the Edwards Opera House to receive their diplomas.

Postal employees took time out of their busy routines to pose for this photograph in front of their workplace. Before 1912, when its present building was constructed on the corner of Seventeenth Street and Main Street, the post office was located at 1812 Main Street. This photograph was taken around 1910; before 1905, Main Street was known as Johnson Avenue. The suite next door housed a wide variety of businesses. (Courtesy of the Parsons Post Office.)

The Elks Theatre was located at Eighteenth Street and Broadway Avenue and was one of the largest structures in town. In 1914, the theater was sold. As the Orpheum, it became a venue for the vaudeville circuit, and later it screened silent films. By far the town's largest public entertainment space when it was constructed, the theater seated 1,200 and contained a wraparound double balcony. Studio Grand created this image.

There were not many men to warm the bench if all members of the 1908–1909 Parsons High School basketball team were present when the photographer composed this formal team photograph. The six-man team, along with its coach, is shown in what would today be considered basic uniforms. The sport of basketball was only 17 years old when this photograph was taken.

The first Parsons High School building was constructed in 1893. Before that time, high school classes were conducted at McKinley School. The high school cost $30,000 and was located at Twenty-sixth Street and Main Street. It served the city in its original capacity for a little over 30 years. When the high school/junior college building was constructed on Main Street in the late 1920s, the old high school became West Junior High School.

Schoolchildren from the second ward, Garfield, show their patriotic spirit in this World War I–era photograph. Although their salutes show varying degrees of competency, the photograph illustrates how the war impacted all ages. The document held by the young soldier on the right-hand side is probably a war bond.

This photograph was taken shortly after Garfield Elementary School was constructed in 1903. Located at approximately the same site as the present elementary school, Fourteenth Street and Corning Avenue, this facility was the second school to bear the name. The first Garfield was built in 1872 at Seventeenth Street and Main Street. When the second Garfield was constructed in 1903, the old school became Parsons City Hall.

It is hard to imagine their uniforms did much to help the agility of the 1917 Parsons High School girls' basketball team, but they remained a stylish ninesome. More than likely, the bowed, turbanlike headgear helped keep the girls' long hair in place. A few years later, the bobbed look became fashionable. However, several girls are wearing wristwatches, a new way to wear timepieces, which were previously pinned to clothing.

When it comes to uniform styles, what a difference several decades make. By the late 1920s or early 1930s when this photograph was taken, the Parsons High School track team wore matching outfits that were not only functional but also fashionable. Based on the number of trophies on the table in front of them, the winged P emblem was an apt symbol of their combined athleticism.

While this photograph was taken to document the progress on the construction of the Parsons Post Office, it does much more than show the basement walls nearing completion. The photograph looks southwest, and it provides rare views of both the Southwestern Bell Telephone building and the Elks Theatre. (Courtesy of the Parsons Post Office.)

A solitary figure surveys the future site of the Parsons Post Office, lots 1–6, block 32, located at 1700–1710 Main Street. The federal government began buying the lots in January 1909. At the time this photograph was taken, probably in 1911, Parsons streetcars, which were the predecessors of the interurban, traveled Main Street, and the east end of the 1800 block of Main Street was vacant. (Courtesy of the Parsons Post Office.)

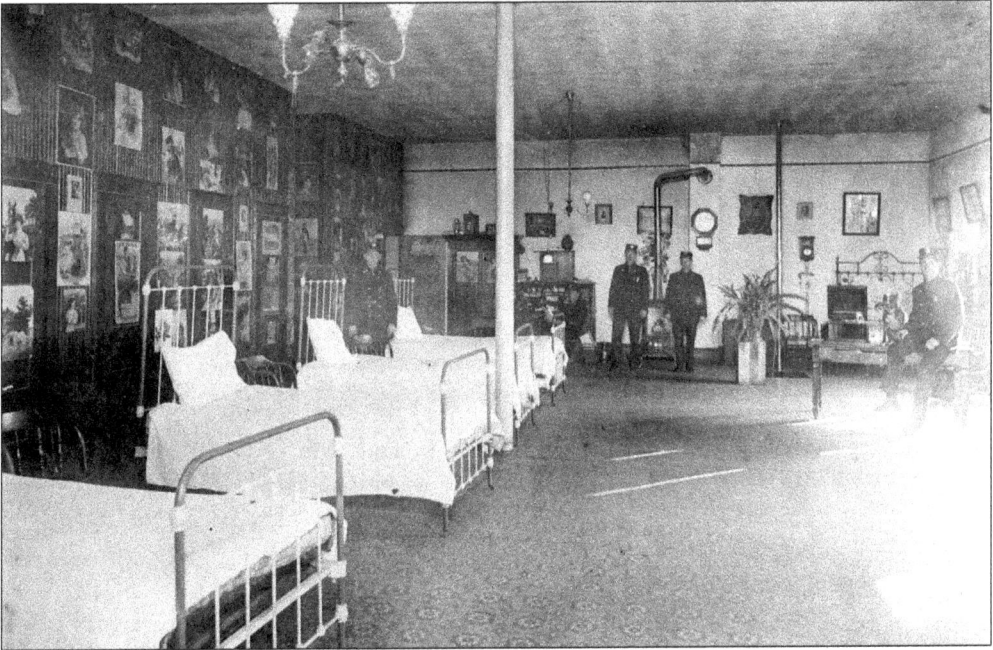

This 1911 photograph affords a rare peek at the sleeping quarters of the Parsons Fire Department. The fireman on the right-hand side of the photograph poses with what is probably the firehouse dog, a boxer. The wall behind the row of beds is adorned with poster art mostly featuring young women.

Free coffee, sandwiches, and fruit were available to soldiers at the Red Cross canteen during World War I; doughnuts were added to the menu during World War II. The canteen was located between the Katy passenger station and its companion, the Katy office building. This photograph dates from the World War I era.

Members of the Parsons Fire Department pose for this photograph on November 16, 1916. Taken by the Morris Electric Studio, the photograph captures most of the 1800 block of Washington Avenue, including Parker's Livery Stable and Shelby Cuddy's Garage. J. M. Womeldorff was proprietor of the Metropolitan Stable, an establishment that advertised high-class livery and

City officials pose for this photograph taken in 1923, shortly after the Parsons Municipal Building was completed. Built in the beaux arts style, the building is typical of 1920s civic auditoriums, although the decision to use a lighter-colored brick was probably considered avant-garde at the time. Even though the World War I memorial, the doughboy statue, had yet to make an

boarding with special attention paid to rigs for picnic parties and funeral wagons. The Parsons Fire Department remains in this location, although the buildings that surround the facility have changed, most notably after the 1959 bowling alley fire and the April 2000 tornado.

UILDING CITY OFFICERS Parsons Kans. 1923

appearance on the northwest corner of the lawn, most of the area, including the two residences south of the auditorium, remains much the same as it was when the photograph was taken 85 years ago. The view looks southeast from Seventeenth Street.

The Katy Athletic Field, located west of the Katy shops at Twenty-fifth Street and Dirr Avenue, was the scene of many high school games. This contest between Chanute and Parsons High Schools took place on November 30, 1916, a few weeks after the field was officially dedicated. The dedication itself, which drew an estimated 12,000 people who traveled to and from the field by streetcar, was a major event in the history of the city.

The Parsons Sunflower Band was just one of several social organizations formed by Katy Railroad employees. The band members, from the railroad clerk's union, were active in community events, often sponsoring floats in annual parades and playing at city functions. This photograph captures the band on a summer's day, most likely in Forest Park.

Members of the Parsons High School drum corps and band pose on the front lawn of the high school and junior college building on Main Street. When the building was opened in 1927, it was one of the largest in the state of Kansas. The girls' high school drum corps, under the direction of Charles S. "Pop" McCray, was the first in the nation. Although the exterior of the building remains much the same as it was in the photograph, in 2000, the building underwent a multimillion-dollar renovation. It now houses Parsons Middle School.

Mercy Hospital was built in 1913 and was operated by the Sisters of St. Joseph of Wichita. Because the population of Parsons swelled with the opening of the Kansas Ordnance Plant during World War II, a larger facility was needed. Thus, in 1943 an addition to the original hospital was constructed. Mercy Hospital remained in operation until 1961 when the Labette County Medical Center opened.

Someone at the Kansas Electric Power Company had a green thumb, if this August 1924 photograph is any indication. The facility, which still stands at Twenty-first Street and Morton Avenue, looks much the same today minus the elaborate landscaping. The carefully tended flower beds include elephant ears, cannas, and petunias.

According to the 1927 *Juconian*, the Parsons Junior College yearbook, the Red Peppers was the only organized pep club at the college. It promoted school spirit at both basketball and football games. The group was formed in 1926 and was partially sponsored by Rotary International. This photograph features members of the flapper-era group in their trademark red and white striped blazers. They rode on the "Red Baby," the official Red Pepper car. So distinctive were their outfits that images of the school mascot, the cardinal, were drawn with the cardinal clad in his own striped coat.

The Kansas Gas and Electric plant, located on the Neosho River east of Parsons, was a state-of-the-art facility that became a source of pride to area residents. These two 1930 Morris Studio photographs show the facility in its early prime. Employees of the plant pose with the company bus. The swinging bridge over the Neosho River was a fondly remembered structure, often populated by youth who were thrilled by sneaking across it despite the No Trespassing/For Employees Only sign that was clearly posted. One area resident remembers riding her bicycle across the bridge.

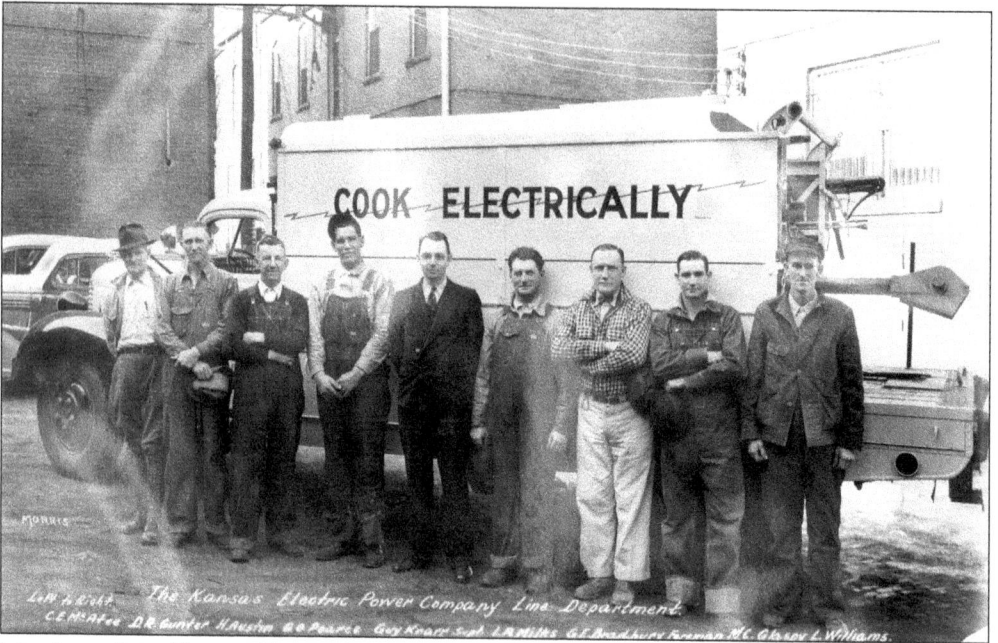

Members of the Kansas Electric Power Company line department pose for this Morris Studio photograph, probably taken in the 1940s. While many housewives across the country were cooking with gas, Kansas Electric Power Company had a different message and a snappy graphic to illustrate it: "Cook Electrically."

This snapshot captures a group of McKinley School students in front of the partially completed building. The first McKinley School was constructed in 1874; additions were made in 1890 and in 1912. This photograph dates from 1935. McKinley School was closed late in the 20th century. The building was heavily damaged by the 2000 tornado, but it survived the storm.

Although the first YMCA was organized by the city in 1885, by 1907, the Katy Railroad and the city assumed joint sponsorship of the facility. A major building project in 1916 resulted in the YMCA that most people remember. Located at 2005 Broadway Avenue, it featured dormitory and recreation rooms, a swimming pool, a gymnasium, and a bowling alley. In the summer of 1936 when this photograph was taken, the building was 20 years old.

The girls' swimming class of 1930 is captured in this YMCA photograph. While the pool appears a tad dismal by today's aquatic standards, it was nevertheless a huge asset to the community, and generations of Parsons's youth posed for similar photographs. In contrast to the exposed pipes, the pool was decorated with ornate tile and for many years was the only indoor pool in Parsons.

There is a wide range of expressions on the faces of law enforcement officers as members of the Parsons Police Department pose for this formal portrait in December 1949. Thirteen of those pictured are uniformed officers; the two men in street clothes are probably detectives or supervisors.

Parking meters were already a fixture of downtown Parsons by the 1950s, as this photograph of the Southwestern Bell Telephone building illustrates. The Parsons Recreation Commission later made the building its home. It was located at 1711 Broadway Avenue near the Parsons Carnegie Library and Elks Theatre. This building was the center of the telephone company's operations for over 50 years.

During World War II, one of the major employers in the city was the Kansas Ordnance Plant, which consisted of over 400 buildings on 17,000 acres of land east of Parsons. This photograph, one of a series taken in August 1943, is labeled, "Seat primer and stamp cartridge case."

In its first three years of operation, the Kansas Ordnance Plant produced over a million tons of ammunition, most of it shipped to Africa and the southwest Pacific. Security was tight during World War II, and it was not until the end of the war that the general public was allowed to view the facility at an open house on September 22, 1945. Plant personnel took this photograph on August 9, 1943. Its caption reads, "75 MM Shell. Overall picture of 75MM propellant charge loading bay."

Residents of Parsons were among the first in the state to enjoy the wonders of cable television. The system was greeted with much excitement, and the citywide festivities were captured in a series of photographs by Leon Crooks. None other than the reining Miss America, Deborah Bryant, was in town to promote the system. Local pageant winners greeted her at the Parsons Tri-City Airport. The Troposcatter antenna, which pulled channels from Kansas City and Topeka, was located approximately two miles south of Parsons on Tenth Street. Monroe Rifkin (left) and Bob Rhodes pose in front of the antenna, which was used for only a few years. Those who visited the site reported that the wires, an unexpected addition to the open sky, took the life of many birds.

# Six

# CHALLENGES AND DISASTERS

While they are difficult to spot, firemen are on the scene of the Katy depot fire. Residents throughout the city used every means of available transportation to view the fire firsthand. This C. E. Cadmus photograph shows the north end of the depot. The St. Clair Hotel and Café, located on the south side of the 1900 block of Main Street, is visible on the left-hand side of the photograph.

Although it may have been straight-line winds or a microburst spawned by an intense thunderstorm, the handwritten notation on this photograph blamed a cyclone for the destruction of the original Katy shops. Katy workers pose in front of the wreckage in this photograph, dated 1903.

Another view of the Katy shops illustrates the extent of the damage done by the August 1903 cyclone. There was no extensive damage reported in other parts of the city, but Katy employees had a lot of work to do to clean the area of the tangled iron that remained after the storm.

Sightseers visit the Bender home, which was located west of Parsons on the Osage Mission-Fort Scott Road, the site of the nation's first recorded mass murders. The Bender family purchased the farm in 1870; by 1873, at least 75 travelers were reported missing. Many of them were making their way west along the road that passed near the Bender home. After the discovery of 10 bodies on the site, the farm became a tourist attraction. One local newspaper reported that over 3,000 people visited the site on Sunday May 15, 1873. The sandstone rock that served as a stepping stone into their home is located in the Parsons Historical Society Museum.

A group of soldiers is pictured in front of the makeshift hospital site. During World War I, Parsons was home to the Kansas Field Hospital No. 2, which was located north of the YMCA building. This rare photograph captures the day-to-day domesticity and the primitive nature of the facility. The warehouse owned by the Ellis and Martin Furniture Store and Undertaking establishment is visible in the next block to the north on Main Street.

One of the most devastating fires in Parsons was the one that took place on November 13, 1907. Although it is commonly known as the First Baptist Church fire, the fire spread quickly, and several blocks of downtown structures were destroyed. Reports at the time blamed boys playing with fire in a barn. This image looks southeast toward city hall, which stood where the Parsons Municipal Building now stands. The view covers the 1700 block of Main Street and the 1700 block of Washington Avenue. Damage at the time was estimated at $100,000.

Another view of the November 13, 1907, fire looks northwest and was probably taken from an upper story of the city hall building. St. Patrick's Catholic Church and Central Avenue Christian Church are visible in the distance. The two intersecting streets in the foreground are Seventeenth Street and Main Street.

Fire destroyed several buildings on the south side of the 1800 block of Broadway Avenue on April 29, 1909. This Studio Grand photograph captures the collapse of a wall as onlookers stand nearby. While the photographer's attention was clearly focused on the fire, modern viewers may notice the iron hitching posts that lined Broadway Avenue. Studio Grand was located just east of the burned buildings. The view below shows the aftermath of the blaze, looking north across Broadway Avenue. To keep pedestrians away from the below-street-level debris, a temporary wood barrier was constructed. The ornate building in the middle of the photograph contains the names of two businesses from around 1900, Wilkin and Company and George Haines.

The Katy depot was less than 20 years old when it caught fire on March 18, 1912. A strong east wind fanned the flames, and the station burned to the ground. At the time, as many as 30 passenger trains a day were using the facility. Because all railroad-related records were lost in the fire, when the station was rebuilt, a separate facility housed the offices and company records.

When fire destroyed the Strasburger building on December 28, 1918, the *Parsons Sun* reported the event as the biggest fire in Parsons's history. The city had lost, at least temporarily, one of its largest businesses. Accounts of the fire at the time blamed the destruction on inadequate water pressure; firemen were unable to fight the fire above the second floor of the four-story building. When owners rebuilt on the same site at the northeast corner of Eighteenth and Main Streets, the new building had two stories.

Curious townspeople inspect what is left of the stucco structure that was St. John's Episcopal Church. Only the altar remained undamaged in the natural gas explosion that destroyed the edifice on September 16, 1916. St. John's was rebuilt on the same location at Eighteenth Street and Corning Avenue. A faulty gas-fired furnace was blamed for the explosion.

The First Baptist Church was destroyed by fire in December 1940. When it was rebuilt at the same location north of the Parsons Municipal Building, the stone-columned facade was incorporated into the new structure. It was all that remained of the old building after the fire. The distinctive dome of the old church, however, was not duplicated. This fire marked the second time that the church's congregation had lost a building to fire. Thirty-three years earlier, in 1907, fire had destroyed a much smaller church building.

This dramatic night view shows the intensity of the blaze that destroyed the Orpheum Theatre on December 20, 1939. By the time the fire was extinguished, the four-story building was a partially collapsed shell. The theater was not rebuilt, and the corner lot, a prime downtown location, was empty for over a decade. In 1954, the Parsonian Hotel was constructed on the site.

Bricks from the west and south walls of the Orpheum Theatre block Eighteenth Street and Broadway Avenue the morning after the blaze. However, the theater's marquee, a twisted victim of the intense heat generated by the blaze, remains attached to the front of the building. The building that housed the theater was two days short of its 35th birthday when fire destroyed it. It was one of the most distinctive and largest buildings in the downtown area. Shortly after the fire, newspapers reported that bricks from the theater were to be incorporated into the new Marvel Park grandstand.

Fire engulfed the Parsons Theatre on September 23, 1943, as 750 people watched the Technicolor movie *White Savage*, starring Jon Hall, Maria Montez, and Sabu. There were no injuries, although a projectionist had to be rescued by firemen. The partially destroyed theater was rebuilt shortly thereafter. Over 50 years later, fire once again broke out in the theater, this time destroying it.

This photograph captures the aftermath of a fire at the Parsons State Hospital on January 5, 1942. Although firefighters and onlookers left the scene by the time this photograph was taken, the photographer, perched atop a nearby tiled-roofed building, captured the fire's devastation and the damage to the nearby building. A single ladder, resting against the building, is visible on the left-hand side of the photograph.

Smoke fills the air near the second-story windows as firemen pour water on the blaze at Cole's Department Store. Damage to the store, which was located at 1730 Main Street, was estimated at a quarter of a million dollars. The structure was built in 1892 to house Steele Hardware, and it has been the home of several businesses, among them Newberry's. The March 1950 blaze was one of several that plagued downtown in the 1940s and 1950s.

A crowd gathers to watch the demise of the Parsons Poultry and Egg Company. Despite the best efforts of the Parsons Fire Department and the presence of state-of-the-art ladders and other modern firefighting equipment, flames engulfed the structure, which was located at 2101 Washington Avenue, on June 15, 1946.

92

Floodwaters surround the Kansas Gas and Electric plant east of Parsons. The facility, located on the Neosho River, has survived several major floods. This picture was taken on July 25, 1948. It looks northwest. Other major floods along the Neosho River took place in 1951 and in 2007.

Trees along a residential street bend under the weight of a coat of ice. Parts of the city were without power for several days during the ice storm of 1949. Based on this photograph, the storm also brought several inches of sleet and snow. While storms of this type are not uncommon, those who remember the 1949 storm use it as the standard to judge all others.

The owners of the Midwest Auto Stores were not taking any chances with their merchandise when fire broke out in the bowling alley two buildings east of their store. Firefighters fought the blaze on March 24, 1959. The bowling alley was located next door to the fire station. The automobile supply store was on the corner of Central Avenue and Washington Avenue.

Dark smoke filled the skies when Alderman's Hardware Store was destroyed by fire in December 1952. The store was located at 3503 Main Street. The farm equipment parked near the building was not damaged in the blaze.

The F3 tornado that struck Parsons in April 2000 destroyed several historic downtown buildings, including the three-story Gregory building on Main Street. This photograph was taken two days after the storm, when most debris had been removed from the streets. The view looks northwest on Central Avenue between Washington Avenue and Crawford Avenue. The Mecca Hotel once occupied the corner where the Elks building now stands. The building destroyed by the tornado was a storage facility at the time. Many years before, it had been the home of Wilson's Five and Ten Cent Store.

The new Parsons Theatre was opened with much fanfare and to public acclaim in March 2000. Less than six weeks later, it was in ruins, one of the most visible victims of the 2000 tornado. The owners rebuilt the theater at the same location on the 200 block of North Seventeenth Street.

Because the 2000 tornado damaged many of the structures that made up the downtown plaza, city officials decided to reopen Main and Eighteenth Streets to traffic. The last vestiges of the plaza were removed approximately 30 years after its conception. This view, taken during the reconstruction of Main Street, looks west near Eighteenth Street.

Main Street is once again the pride of Parsons, as this contemporary photograph illustrates. In 2006, the city was awarded the Great American Main Street Award. This view looks west from the 1700 block of Main Street. The Parsons Post Office is on the left-hand side of the photograph.

# Seven

# THE KATY RAILROAD

The 1895 Missouri-Kansas-Texas Railroad depot was one of the most photographed structures in Parsons. At least 10 different views can be found on penny postcards. However, none shows the structure better than this image, which was often duplicated on china and engraved in the bowls of sterling souvenir spoons. The depot burned to the ground 17 years after it was built.

Before the Missouri-Kansas-Texas Railroad was known as the Katy, it was the Union Pacific Southern Branch. This photograph shows the *Prairie Queen*, the private car that was built in 1870 for Katy general manager Robert Smith Stevens. The car cost $8,000. Although Parsons was named for the president of the Katy, Judge Levi Parsons, Stevens probably did more than any other man to shape the destiny of the town.

The Parsons and Pacific Railroad depot was a frame structure located near Twentieth Street and Belmont Avenue, and as this photograph illustrates, it was within a few feet of the track that passed through Parsons. While the depot was constructed on-site, many of the early buildings in Parsons were moved to the town from nearby settlements.

On May 1, 1886, townspeople gather near the Parsons and Pacific Railroad tracks to celebrate expanded rail service. J. F. Standiford, one of Parsons's early photographers, captured the scene as the first train from Mound Valley arrived in Parsons. While the Katy enterprise dominated rail service, several other railroads, including the Frisco and the Parsons and Pacific, were very much a part of Parsons's past. The wagon near the railroad car is a taxi from the Sherman House, an early hotel.

Missouri-Kansas-Texas Railroad foundry workers pose for a photograph in 1893. The Katy shops at one time included a blacksmith shop, a machine shop, a car repair shop, a store, a power plant, a locomotive repair shop, a freight house, and other support facilities.

By the 1880s, strikes began to plague the Katy Railroad. By far the most serious one took place in 1886. This photograph shows the crowd that gathered along a main street in Parsons on April 11, 1886, as the Kansas National Guard paraded down the street. Even by today's standards, the military presence was striking, and no doubt the sheer number of troops contributed to the quick collapse of the 1886 rail strike. This photograph also provides modern viewers with a sense of the diverse downtown business community at the time, including stables, lumberyards, clothing stores, and candy shops.

The 1886 strike began at 10:00 a.m. on March 6, and it encompassed the entire Katy line. So intense were the animosities between labor and management that rumors surfaced of impending plans to burn the town and to dynamite the Katy shops. In response to the threat, National Guard troops arrived in Parsons on April 2. Within hours, the 1st Regiment of the Kansas National Guard spread across town and began to guard the city and rail facilities. Within the week, the strike was broken, and several of the leaders were arrested and convicted of criminal activity.

It was a cold, snowy day in March when this crowd gathered as part of the Missouri-Kansas-Texas Railroad strike that began 23 days earlier. The handwritten notation on this 1886 photograph reads, "The 'Strike' and how they did it in Parsons, Kas. Monday, Mar. 29th 1886." Three days later, the governor declared martial law, and Kansas National Guardsmen arrived in town.

The winter weather that accompanied much of the strike is more evident in this photograph taken by photographer J. F. Standiford. Although the early spring storm did not bring much snow, it was enough to cover the roofs of homes, and a strong wind added to the general discomfort of strikers.

The first Missouri-Kansas-Texas Railroad freight office had a tile roof, although it was a frame structure. This photograph shows employees in front of the building, which was located at 2001 Crawford Avenue near where the present Union Pacific Railroad office now stands. This image was probably taken around the dawn of the 20th century.

Work began on the construction of the Katy locomotive shop in February 1907. By far the largest of Katy facilities in Parsons, it contained 129,000 square feet and was 150 feet wide and 860 feet long. The total cost of the facility was nearly a third of a million dollars. By July, just six months after construction began, the building was complete. It still stands north of Dirr Avenue and east of Twenty-fifth Street.

The new Missouri-Kansas-Texas Railroad station was completed in 1914, less than two years after fire claimed the Victorian depot. Kansas governor George H. Hodges and C. E. Schaff, president of the Katy, attended the opening ceremonies that were sponsored by the chamber of commerce. The depot was an impressive building, a fitting symbol for the largest freight terminal west of Chicago and one that handled 50,000 to 60,000 cars a month. The newsstand inside the depot was open 24 hours a day, seven days a week.

To the untrained eye, this interior overview of the old Katy shops looks like a jumble of steel and indistinguishable mechanical equipment. However, to railroad enthusiasts, it is an effective research tool, allowing them a glimpse of the workplace that over 200 men populated on a daily basis. The shop opened in 1907, and by 1909, shop employees worked nine hours a day, six days a week.

Today Crawford Avenue is one of the busiest streets in Parsons; when this photograph was taken on November 7, 1919, traffic was considerably lighter. The view looks west. Even then, however, motorists and pedestrians alike were cautioned to "look out for the cars."

Originally, the Missouri-Kansas-Texas Railroad power plant supplied electricity for all railroad operations in Parsons, including the shops, the roundhouse, the offices, and the yards. This Morris Electric Studio photograph illustrates the size of the facility, approximately 60 feet wide by 170 feet long, and focuses on the bank of switchboards beneath the arched windows. When the plant became operational, officials boasted that the plant could supply power for 50,000 people.

A crowd gathered on July 4, 1925, to watch a boxing match at the Katy Athletic Field. Proceeds from the match went to the Katy band. Throughout the 1920s and 1930s, the field hosted a variety of events, including the system-wide Katy Athletic Meet and the Southeast Kansas Baseball Championship. The system-wide meet in 1925 brought 5,000 visitors to Parsons.

The Katy Athletic Field at Twenty-fifth Street and Dirr Avenue was the scene for a team photograph featuring members of the Missouri-Kansas-Texas Railroad stores baseball team. As early as 1917, professional teams such as the Minneapolis Millers, the St. Louis Cardinals, and the Kansas City Blues played exhibition games at the facility. The Katy shops are in the background.

Although there is no record of the specific occasion for which this Electric Studio photograph was taken, the distinguished gentleman who has his back turned to the camera and his hands clasped behind his back seems to have the undivided attention of Katy workers during a shop meeting in 1925. The attention of the other segment of the audience, the coat-clad women, is less singular.

Hundreds of Katy employees gathered for a group photograph by Parsons photographer Ed Peterson. The brick building on the right-hand side of the photograph was the Katy power plant. Although there is no record of the occasion that promoted this photograph, it was probably a picture of all shop employees on duty that day.

This photograph was taken from the roof of the 1914 Missouri-Kansas-Texas Railroad depot and looks across the building that once housed the American Express office. The view is to the north. Although the depot itself was constructed of stone and brick with a steel frame, the office building, located to the south of the depot, was wood with a stucco shell. It was torn down after 1957 along with the mechanical building and the old foundry as part of the railroad's reorganization plan.

Based on the size of the equipment these men are operating, it was probably a good idea that they follow the posted warnings. This 1942 picture shows employees in the Missouri-Kansas-Texas Railroad blacksmith shop. The original shop was constructed in 1907 at a cost of $50,000; another $26,000 was spent to equip the site.

Post–World War II prosperity is very much in evidence as a group of well-dressed grade-school children and their teachers visit the Katy yards and pose with Engine 375. This photograph is dated 1947. The children were members of the third and fourth grades at Garfield Elementary School.

Few towns the size of Parsons could have boasted a railroad complex as extensive or as elaborate as the Katy facility. This photograph, taken in the early 1950s by photographer Leon Crooks, shows the west side of both the depot, constructed in 1914 at a cost of $150,000, and the general office building, built the next year as a companion facility for $50,000. The original decor in the dining room of the depot featured the state seals of Missouri, Kansas, and Texas painted in oils by a Chicago artist.

*Eight*

# PERSONALITIES
# AND PROJECTS

The handwritten notation on the back of this photograph reads, "Buggy load of Parsons pioneer boosters ready to make a trip to Arkansas." While the original caption does not identify all the men, those familiar with early Parsons history will recognize many of the names: M. F. Kohler, O. H. Stewart, W. H. Martin, W. C. Holmes, E. B. Stevens, J. F. Steele, E. H. Edwards, W. L. Bartlett, C. H. Kimball, J. M. Gregory, and C. A. Rasbach.

It is hard to underestimate the influence that Robert Smith "Colonel Bob" Stevens had on the development of Parsons. He is credited with creating the coalition of investors that funded the original Katy enterprise, and he personally planned much of the original settlement. It was Stevens who notified Katy general headquarters in Sedalia, Missouri, that the railroad had reached Oklahoma Territory: "We've struck the territory line and are going like hell."

This formal portrait of Angell Matthewson conveys the strength of character that many of his contemporaries associated with the man. The owner of the Matthewson Hotel, the largest and most luxurious of Parsons's hotels, Matthewson also built what was generally acknowledged as the finest residence in town. It was located on the south side of the 1500 block of Morgan Avenue.

This portrait of C. H. Kimball was probably taken during his tenure in the Kansas legislature. Kimball was active in politics and business in the 1880s and 1890s. In addition to serving on the Labette County Republican Central Committee for many years, he was closely associated with the First National Bank, and he lent his name to several buildings in downtown Parsons.

The Lambert and Duffy Clothing Store was located on the southwest corner of Central Avenue and Main Street when this photograph was taken in 1903. As owners of one of the most fashion-forward shops in Parsons, Charles Lambert (left) and Pete Duffy (right) catered to those interested in style as well as quality garments. Early advertisements indicated that the shop also encouraged high school- and college-age men and women to shop at their establishment: "We will dress you for graduation and do it right." Team Bank now occupies this location.

R. H. Cloughley Automobile Works was located at 2309 Broadway Avenue. While the name certainly sounded impressive, the works was really a shed or barn behind the Cloughley residence. For a short time from 1902 until 1905, he made a very limited number of horseless carriages. Two types were available: gas or steam powered. Both models had a steering option: tiller or wheel. This photograph of a Cloughley car was taken in the late 1970s at a car show.

One of the most prolific photographers in Parsons was William Morris. The Morris Studio, sometimes identified as the Morris Electric Studio, was responsible for capturing much of the history of Parsons during the early part of the 20th century. This 1920s photograph features Morris and his wife, Nola, in front of the studio, which was located at 609 South Thirteenth Street.

T. Claude Ryan was born in Parsons on January 3, 1893. When he was a young man, airplanes and air travel fascinated him. By 1922, Ryan was in San Diego, where he founded the Ryan Flying Company, the first all-year airplane passenger service in California. In 1926, his company produced the M-1 mail plane, the first production monoplane. However, it was his contributions to the flight of Charles Lindbergh's *Spirit of St. Louis* that are most remembered. The Ryan Flying Company designed and built the plane, which was officially known as the Ryan NYP.

This 1920s photograph of the interior of the Peterson Studio was undoubtedly intended as publicity for the business. While the majority of the photographs displayed are portraits, Peterson took his camera around town, often capturing events as they happened. Photographs of parades, fires, and civic activities all bear the distinctive Peterson Studio seal. The studio was located at 1817½ Main Street.

Charles S. "Pop" McCray taught orchestra and band at Parsons High School and Parsons Junior College. His brother Walter was the second director of the music department at Pittsburg State University. McCray organized the first girls' marching drum corps in the United States, and under his direction, music at Parsons High School was made a part of the academic curriculum not an extracurricular activity. Much beloved by several generations of students, he inspired many with his love of music.

Rees H. Hughes began his tenure as superintendent of the Parsons schools in 1922, a position he held for 20 years. During that time, he was instrumental in establishing Parsons Junior College. The college's yearbook, the *Juconian*, praised his dedication to excellence and noted that Hughes was both admired and revered by junior college students. Hughes later became president of Kansas State Teacher's College at Pittsburg and a member of the state legislature. Rees Hughes Field, the former high school athletic field and the site of Parsons's only band shell, was named in his honor. Today the Rees Hughes Center at the same site (now Parsons Middle School) honors Hughes's contributions to education. (Courtesy of the Hughes family.)

Nelly Don was one of the most successful dress manufacturers in the world. She was born Ellen Howard Quinlan in Parsons, one of 13 children. Her father was a farmer and worked in the Missouri-Kansas-Texas Railroad shops. After she graduated from Parsons High School, Don attended Parsons Business College before moving to Kansas City. By 1931, the Nelly Don Company employed 1,000 workers and made 5,000 dresses a day. During World War II, the company was the largest manufacturer of women's military and work clothes in the country. A film about Don, *Nelly Don: A Stitch in Time*, premiered in Kansas City in 2006. (Courtesy of the Nelly Don Collection of Terence and Heather O'Malley.)

ZaSu Pitts was born in Parsons on January 3, 1894. When she was nine, the family moved to Santa Cruz, California. Although known for her comedic performances in films of the 1930s and 1940s, Pitts was a star on Broadway and on television, appearing with Gale Storm on the *Oh, Susannah! Show*. In silent films, she starred in the Eric von Stroheim classic *Greed*. A granite star at the entrance to the Parsons Theatre notes her accomplishments.

Many people name Dale Hall, No. 88 in this photograph, as the greatest athlete to emerge from the Parsons sports program. Hall, the only Parsons High School football player to have his number retired, was first-team all-state in football and basketball both his junior and senior years, the only Kansan to hold that honor. At the United States Military Academy at West Point, Hall was a member of the 1944 national championship team, and he played with two Heisman Trophy winners. For three years from 1959 to 1961, he coached West Point's football team. This 1942 photograph shows the Parsons High School team in front of the band shell at Rees Hughes Field.

Wilber Dorsey "Buck" Clayton, one of the country's premier jazz trumpeters, was born in Parsons on November 12, 1911. After graduating from Parsons High School, he moved to Los Angeles. Clayton, who once played with the Count Basie Orchestra, had an extensive recording career, toured internationally, and occasionally appeared in film. *Buck Clayton's Jazz World*, an autobiography, was published in 1986. This photograph was taken on the Parsons Plaza when Clayton was in Parsons promoting his book. (Used by permission of the University of Missouri Kansas City Libraries, Dr. Kenneth J. LaBudde Department of Special Collections.)

For many years, the Leon Crooks Studio was located at 1807 Main Street and later at 73 Parsons Plaza. Crooks first worked for Parsons photographer Don Peterson, but in 1958, he bought the business and opened his own studio, which featured a cursive neon sign that was one of the most distinctive on Main Street. This photograph, which features a window display of Parsons's pastors, was probably taken around Easter. Items from Crooks's studio, probably the last of the great Parsons photography studios, are located in the Leon Crooks Room of the Parsons Historical Society Museum.

First Car Through Subway Parsons, Kan.

One of the largest engineering projects in Parsons's early history was the subway that allowed interurban and trolley cars to pass beneath the Katy tracks while still allowing wagons and pedestrians street-level access across the rail line in the heart of downtown. This Peterson photograph shows the first car to use the subway even though work on the project looks far from complete. This photograph was probably taken in 1913.

Nine men and one woman pose on the first streetcar on the railway in Parsons. This photograph of the occasion must have been for publicity purposes, as the car does not look passenger friendly. Later cars were more elaborate and more like traditional streetcars. The Kress store, which was located on the 1700 block of Main Street, is in the background.

The owners of the first streetcar on the electric railroad misspelled the name of the town, but no one on the streetcar seems to mind. This Studio Grand photograph captures the excitement and pride of those aboard for the ride. The first railcars were horse drawn or were powered by hand pumps; the electric streetcar came later and was eventually integrated into the interurban system.

The Stars and Stripes waves above the site of the new Katy station. Rail officials wasted no time in rebuilding the depot after the 1912 fire. This photograph looks east from across the tracks. The two large brick buildings behind the iron framework are the Elks Theatre—later the Orpheum Theatre—and Parsons Business College, once the site of Parsons's first library.

Business in downtown Parsons in general and on Main Street in particular was disrupted for months during 1951. That year, the underpass subway was widened from two lanes to four lanes. Businesses that are visible in this view are Ben's Grill, First Federal Savings and Loan, the Kansan Theatre, Sengpheil's Furniture, and the St. Clair Hotel.

The YMCA building was one of several that fell victim to progress in the late 1960s and early 1970s. As part of the urban renewal project, many buildings in the same neighborhood were razed. Once the source of immense civic pride, by the time this photograph was taken, the YMCA building had outlived its usefulness as a recreational facility.

It was truly the end of an era when the venerable Katy station was torn down in April 1972, 58 years and three months after it had opened. Although the station was a long-neglected building when the wrecking crews began their work, many local residents continue to mourn the loss of the depot, once the pride of the Missouri-Kansas-Texas Railroad.

# Nine

# SOUVENIRS

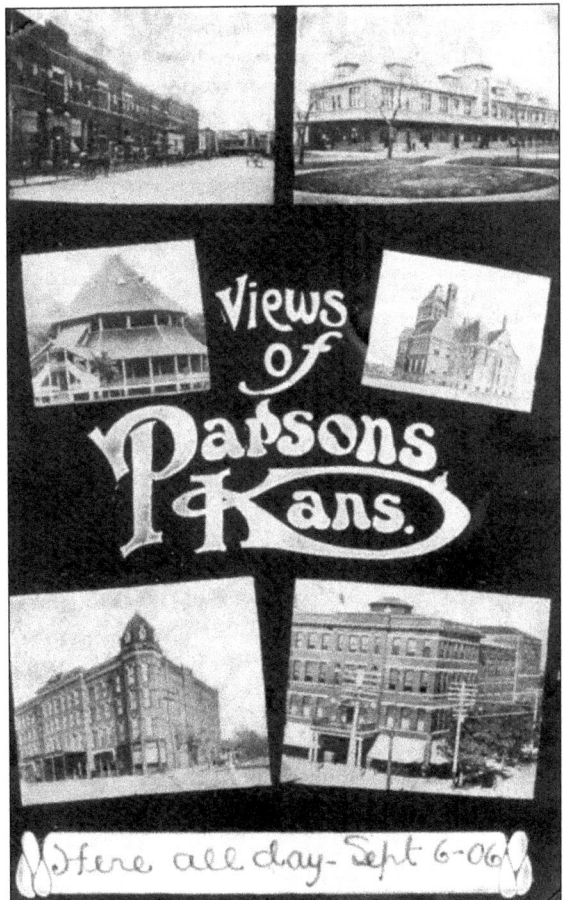

It is easy to date this early multiple-view Parsons postcard. Like the person who originally sent the card, many people in transit found themselves in Parsons for a day, a few hours, or a few minutes, often just long enough to send a card. A traveler sent this message to someone in Topeka: "We never had a bit of trouble changing cars. In fact it was fun."

This postcard image of the Matthewson Hotel is a bit deceiving, at least in terms of its surroundings. The card does not convey the fact that the hotel enjoyed a prime location in the heart of the city. The Frisco depot was directly south across Belmont Avenue, and the Katy station complex was one block to the northwest. One hotel guest wrote, "Matthewson Hotel. Wednesday Evening. Parsons. Arrived here ok. All have a good place to stay across from the Katy Station where you and I ate breakfast."

Less exotic than its name implies, the Mecca Hotel, which was located on the southwest corner of Central Avenue and Crawford Avenue, was among the largest hotels in Parsons. Its economical rates and flexible meal plans probably appealed to budget-minded travelers. A Mecca postcard mailed on August 15, 1910, to Spaulding, Oklahoma, reads, "Wednesday is payday, and I expect we will leave Parsons this week. We are well as usual."

Strasburger's Department Store touted itself as the "Complete Outfitters for Womankind in the State of Kansas." This early postcard is evidence that it did business in nearby states as well. A note written by an employee to a woman in Welch, Oklahoma, is dated March 12, 1910: "As per your request we are sending the waist patterns, but the price of same is .15 cents instead of .10 cents. Please remit at your earliest opportunity as we do not usually charge mail orders."

The Parsons Business College building is one of several structures that dominated the skyline of Parsons around 1900. J. C. Olson, who managed the facility in its heyday, tirelessly promoted the facility, and his efforts were justified. By 1905, it had over 500 students and was recognized as one of the leading business colleges of the West. A postcard dated November 25, 1909, reads, "Arrived in Parsons this morning. Leave at 9 for Dallas, Texas. All are well and slept fine last night in sleeper. We are on the Katy Flyer. Writing this crossing the Arkansas River at this minute."

Several Parsons postcards were extremely popular. Along with photographs of the Katy station and the Elks Theatre, this view of the Forest Park Pavilion was one that many people sent. The structure, typically Victorian in nature, was home to band concerts, dances, and civic events. The pavilion was destroyed by fire in the 1940s. A postcard sent on January 12, 1909, reads, "Your most beautiful card received but owing to the holiday rush in the mail service, I delayed answering. I am one of the city letter carriers, and I was certainly busy there for awhile."

At one time, there were 40 railroad-affiliated hospitals in the United States but only four in Kansas. The Katy Hospital, which was constructed in 1922 and opened in March 1923, was one of those four. Located in the Stevens addition north of Crawford Avenue between Thirtieth and Thirty-first Streets, the hospital was once the sole occupant of the block. It closed in 1985. The Katy Hospital building was recently placed on the National Register of Historic Places.

This multiple-view postcard dates from the 1940s and features a picture of the Mercy Hospital addition. It was mailed to Centerdale, Rhode Island, from Parsons in 1944. The original sender wrote, "At present I am in the U.S.O. Last night we went on a scavenger hunt and had quite a time. My partner and myself had to get a black cat, a girdle, and some nail polish. You should have seen me with the girdle on."

This set of real-photo stamps was probably produced in the 1940s and is quite rare. While it shows a variety of Parsons's landmarks, one photograph of East Junior High School is reproduced twice in the series and once mislabeled as Parsons Senior High School. Material accompanying the stamps urges people to "use on your correspondence and on the back of envelopes. Send the whole set or a single stamp photograph to your friends, showing the interesting and beautiful views. Ask them to mail you stamps of their hometown."

M. K. & T. R. R.
General Office Building & R. R. Station.

This souvenir folder dates from the around 1920. In addition to the image on the cover, it featured 10 other views of Parsons, including ones of Grand and Morgan Avenues, the Matthewson Hotel, Main Street, and the Parsons Carnegie Library. A miniature version of the set, approximately half the size of a standard postcard, was also available. A postcard similar to this one carries the inscription, "This is our new depot. It is just grand inside."

Bird's-eye view postcards were popular because they provided a perspective that most people, even residents of their own communities, rarely saw. This view was probably taken from the roof of the White building; it looks southwest from the 1800 block of Main Street. The building with the small onion-shaped dome was home to the Flynn Morris Clothing Company. It was later remodeled to become the Parsons Theatre.

What became the Frisco line into Parsons was originally known as the Memphis, Kansas, and Colorado Railroad when it was built in the late 1870s. Frisco bought the line and integrated it into its system, which extended locally from Pittsburg to Cherryvale. By 1908, local Frisco advertisements promoted "luxurious observation cars on trips to the beautiful Ozarks and picturesque Southwest."

This aerial view of the Parsons State Hospital grounds shows the facility as it appeared before the major building projects of the late 1950s and 1960s. The new facilities, including cottage-style housing units, gave the complex a more residential feel. Only a few of the original structures, mostly support facilities, remain as they appear in this postcard.

Visit us at
arcadiapublishing.com

www.ingramcontent.com/pod-product-compliance
Lightning Source LLC
Chambersburg PA
CBHW050713110426
42813CB00007B/2175